✳ American Quilts ✳

BOOK 2: HATTIE'S STORY

D0062960

First Aladdin Paperbacks edition December 2000

Text copyright © 2000 by Susan E. Kirby

Aladdin Paperbacks
An imprint of Simon & Schuster
Children's Publishing Division
1230 Avenue of the Americas
New York, NY 10020

Printed and bound in the United States of America

10 9 8 7 6 5 4 3 2 1

Library of Congress Control Number 00-109122

ISBN: 0-689-80970-0

Acknowledgments

Nancy Saul, LifeStyle Editor, *The Courier*
Thank you for sharing the treasure hunt!
Sue Kruger, Mount Hope-Funks Grove Township Library
Your expertise in locating resource books is greatly appreciated.

Research is always a treasure hunt. But it was a joy and a rich find to discover traces of the Underground Railroad so close to home. This book is dedicated to Mount Hope and to those past, present, and future who live by the perfect law that gives freedom.

Dear Reader:

Mount Hope Colony derives its name from Mount Hope, Rhode Island. Its founders hoped to recreate New England farms, villages, and ideals upon the Illinois prairie. For $500, a shareholder received 320 acres of land for raising crops and livestock as well as four lots in the village of Mount Hope.

The original emigrants were Congregationalists and abolitionists. History records five men of Mount Hope Colony as being conductors on the Underground Railroad. It is written that one of these gentlemen often returned home from Bloomington with his clothes splattered in eggs aimed in response to his street corner anti-slavery diatribes.

The Fugitive Slave Act of 1850 increased tensions in a state of divided sympathies as lawmen were authorized to enlist the help of private citizens in pursuing fleeing slaves. One Mount Hope abolitionist was quoted as saying, "They can make me look for fugitives, but they sure can't make me find any."

The ardor of that statement brought the man to life for me, and with him, a family and a community with a story to tell. Weaving Lincoln's Lost Speech into *Hattie's Story* was a labor of love. I'll tell you a little secret, dear reader. When I was a little girl learning to play the piano, I used to pretend Abraham Lincoln was on the edge of his seat, listening. And no, he did *not* poke his fingers in his ears. Not in *my* daydream!

I tell you this to free your pen. Let your imagination run wild and tell a tale that comes from your heart. Family history is a wonderful place to begin. If yours has been lost, paint your own, using history as your canvas, fiction as your palette, and words as your brush.

Happy Reading, Happy Writing.

Susan E. Kirby

✴ American Quilts ✴

BOOK 2: HATTIE'S STORY

✴ ✴ ✴ SUSAN E. KIRBY ✴ ✴ ✴

ALADDIN PAPERBACKS

NEW YORK   LONDON   TORONTO   SYDNEY   SINGAPORE

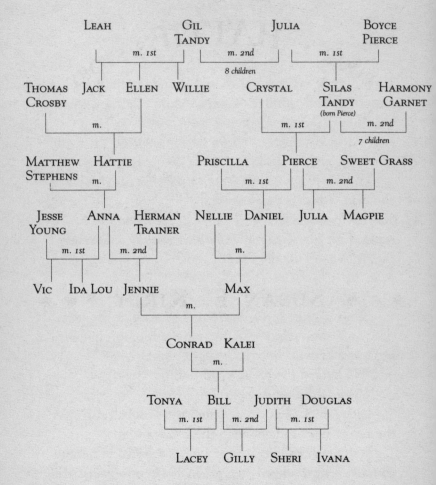

Prologue

Lacey Tandy sat down at the table and poured herself a glass of milk. Beyond the open window, Sheri was shooting hoops. *Thump. Thump. Thump. Swish.*

"Al-l-l r-i-i-i-ght!" Sheri cheered herself on while Ivana banged on the piano in the living room.

"B-flat, Ivana!" called Judith, her back to Lacey as she made toast at the counter.

The coffeemaker hissed. The toaster popped. Judith scraped off black edges while Dad shoveled scrambled eggs into a serving dish on the table. Lacey jumped as he beat the iron skillet with a spoon.

"Let's eat," he called.

Sheri trotted inside and joined Lacey at the table. She wore shorts and a T-shirt, and fanned herself with her baseball cap. "Bacon and eggs? Smells great."

"No hats at the table," said Judith.

"Airmail!" warned Sheri.

Lacey ducked as Sheri sailed the baseball cap over the top of her head and into the living room.

Ivana wandered in, dressed in pink down to her fingernails. She propped her piano book up against the milk jug and hummed the music.

"Get the book off the table, please," said Judith. "Elbows, too."

Lacey moved her elbows while Ivana slid the piano book under her chair. Judith slipped into the chair next to Lacey and took her hand for the blessing. The first tangy bite of orange brought a sting to Lacey's nose. She rubbed her eyes and caught Dad and Judith trading glances over their coffee cups.

"What's wrong?" she asked.

Judith smiled. "Nothing. Life couldn't be better."

"Shall I tell them our secret? Or do you want to?" asked Dad.

"Let them guess," said Judith, face shining.

"Are we moving out to the farm?" asked Lacey. She loved going to her great-grandmother's farm at Funks Grove.

Dad chuckled. "Gram couldn't take much of that."

"A room of my own?" guessed Ivana.

"I hate guessing games," wailed Sheri. "Just tell us."

"Very well, then," said Judith. "I'm expecting."

"A baby?" cried Sheri and Ivana.

Lacey's heart sank, even as her stepsisters squealed in delight. There had been a lot of changes in the year and a half since Dad had remarried—stepsisters, stepmom, space crunch, sonic boom noise level. *And now a baby*.

Where would they put a baby? How would the walls hold any more noise? *What if Dad loved the baby more than he loved her?* Lacey ate her breakfast in silence. She had worked hard to finish her quilt square so she could show Gram today. Why should Judith's news spoil her day at the farm? She wouldn't talk about it. She wouldn't even *think* about it.

Gram Jennie was Dad's grandmother. She and Grampa Max had raised Dad from the time he was twelve because he had wanted to help with the farm after his father was killed in Vietnam and his mother, Gram Kalei, returned to her home state of Hawaii. Lacey enjoyed visiting Gram Kalei in Hawaii. But as it was for Dad, the farm at Funks Grove was her favorite place in the whole world.

Dad dropped Lacey off at the farm on his way to keep an appointment. "Give Gram my love," he said.

"I will!" Lacey climbed out at the edge of the yard and waved as Dad drove away. She raced up the path and inside without knocking. The papered walls in the front room and the parlor beyond were faded. Cracks wiggled across the ceilings. The floors were uneven. But the fine old furniture and Gram's collection of quilts strewn about masked the bumps and bruises left by generations of Tandys who had grown up in this house.

Beyond the doorless arch between the living room and the parlor, Gram sat by the window, sewing. Lacey left Dad and Judith's news on the rug with her muddy shoes. She crept on soundless feet and stopped behind Gram's parlor chair.

"Guess who?" she said, and covered Gram's eyes, glasses and all.

"Eleanor Roosevelt?" guessed Gram. She laughed with Lacey. "No, wait! I know that giggle. It's my Lacey!"

Gram's hair was silvery gray and soft as lamb's wool. It tickled Lacey's cheek as they hugged and kissed. She tasted of face powder and smelled deep pink, like the rose sharing the corner table with a stained-glass lamp and sewing widgets.

"I finished Ellen Tandy." Lacey patted the book bag hanging by a strap from her shoulder. "Do you want to see?"

"But of course," said Gram. "Bring her into the kitchen and we'll have a snack, shall we?"

The raisin cookies were soft and spicy. Gram poured milk into a hand-painted tea cup for Lacey. She looked over the blue sunbonnet girl Lacey had stitched to the white quilt block. It was the first of many such squares to be made. Each sunbonnet girl and overall boy would represent someone on Lacey's family tree. The quilt would warm Lacey on winter nights. It would also help her remember the family stories behind the quilts in Gram's collection.

"How is everyone?" asked Gram.

Lacey told her about school and Sheri practicing for basketball camp and Ivana's new piano teacher. She told her that Judith had had a tooth pulled and that she and Dad had seen a deer on the way out to the farm. But she didn't say a word about the coming baby.

"I'm doing some repairs on a favorite old quilt of mine," said Gram, when Lacey had finished her cookies and milk. "It's ragged. But it has courage stitched into it, and hope and heartache, too."

Lacey hadn't thought of quilts beyond cloth and stitches. "What color is it?" she asked.

"I'll show you." Gram Jennie led the way into the

parlor and her favorite chair. She spread the quilt over her lap. It had tulips on it and stems that crossed. The cloth, yellowed by time, was scorched and stained and patched. A jigsaw puzzle held together with stitches.

"What happened to it?" she asked.

"A lot," said Gram. "It was made in hiding when folks were at odds until no one was safe from the trouble. Not even children."

"What year?"

"1855." Gram pointed out the date and the name *Lizzy* embroidered in one corner. There were two other names, Naomi and Hagar. Lacey didn't recognize any of the three as being family names.

"The trouble had been building for a long, long time. People tried to compromise. But matters only got worse. The problem was the flaw in the fabric that held them together," said Gram.

Lacey had learned a lot about flaws over the past year. Sheri never picked up after herself. Ivana thought she was boss because she was the oldest. And they said she was spoiled from being an only child for so long. Boy, had *that* changed.

"Yoo-hoo, Lacey!" Gram Jennie waved a hand in front of Lacey's face. "Aren't you going to ask me about the flaw?"

Lacey gathered her wandering thoughts and asked, "What was the flaw?"

"On second thought, I'll tell you the story and leave it to you to name the flaw," Gram patted Lacey's blue sunbonnet girl. "Your Ellen here married a fellow from the east named Thomas Crosby. They lived on a farm just a few miles south of here with their daughter Hattie. Hattie was my grandmother. She had a sunny nature. She said so herself. She also told me that as a child, she was good at ducking shadows."

"You knew her, then?"

"Oh, my yes. We were like this." Gram Jennie crossed her middle finger over her forefinger to show how close she had been to her grandmother. "It was she who taught me to sew. She also gave me the family quilts that had passed into her hands over the years."

"And the stories to go with them?" asked Lacey.

"Yes, indeed," said Gram. "Gram Hattie had a wonderful memory for family stories."

"Like you," said Lacey. "Did Hattie make this quilt?"

"No," said Gram. "In fact, she didn't much like sleeping under it."

"How come?"

"She said it let in the darkness," said Gram.

Chapter One

May 1856

Freckled, green-eyed Hattie Crosby was a live spark in a colony of dwindled dreams called Mount Hope. She shook her dark hair and stamped her foot so hard, the ground shook. The covered wagon rolled away, taking her friend Dora June Carlson and the new teacher, Miss Garnet, off to Kansas Territory.

"Stop! Come back, come back!" cried Hattie, running along behind.

The wheels turned. The words shifted and changed into low voices and shuffling feet. The wagon melted away, leaving only a moonlit room. Hattie rolled over in bed and rubbed here eyes.

Sweetbrier arched over the open window. A light breeze breathed its apple-scented fragrance over Hattie's quilt. She smelled meat frying in the next room. But it felt like the dead of night.

Hattie turned on her corn-husk mattress and slept until birds sang and the sky brightened. She dressed and straightened the quilt. It was a repeating tulip pattern, and colorful. The center petals were coffin-shaped and their stems made black crosses.

A careful eye could see the tulips weren't all the

same size. Some of the crosses were longer and thinner than others and the stitches were irregular. It wasn't Mama's usual work, not in craftsmanship and not in color. None of her quilts had black in them. You couldn't buy black cloth at the store. It had to be home-dyed. Hattie didn't remember seeing the quilt made, but she supposed it was when Mama was off her feet, trying to bring a baby to term. Mama was better at finishing quilts than finishing babies.

Hattie's door creaked as she swung it wide. She trotted across the front room and snuggled up to Mama, who was cooking on the stone hearth. Short and round and warm and steamy, Mama was best this way, before the day scratched that quick impatience that lay just below the surface.

"I love you, Mama."

"Sweetness, so early in the morning?" There was wood smoke in Mama's hug, in her hair, and the crush of her calico dress. A scar left by the lash of a whip in childhood play seamed the soot-smudged cheek Hattie kissed.

"Has Poppa eaten already?" asked Hattie.

"No, you're up just right. The porridge is almost ready."

Hattie tilted her turned-up nose. "I thought I smelled meat."

"Not unless a frog stuck his toe in the pot when I was looking the other way."

"I must have dreamed it. I had some gummers." Hattie giggled and told Mama her dream about Miss

Garnet becoming Dora June's mama through marriage.

"It was Poppa talking about Kansas Territory that made me dream it," finished Hattie. "Miss Garnet wouldn't really marry the constable. He's homely as homely can be."

"You better not let Dora June hear you say that. You'll hurt her feelings," warned Mama.

It would, sure enough. Mr. Carlson was a widower. His sister had come up from Kentucky to keep the cabin and look after Dora June. Dora June tolerated Auntie Carlson well enough. But she was flat out devoted to her long-whiskered pa.

Mama gave the pot another stir, then crossed to one side of the fireplace for a skillet. Pegs, driven into the wall, held her collection of iron pots and kettles and pans. Hattie ducked into her apron, tied the strings, and pulled the dining table out from the wall. She lifted one leaf and took the blue-edged dishes from the walnut cupboard.

"I'll finish. Go feed the chickens and gather the eggs," said Mama.

Papa's fields bordered Mount Hope settlement on the north and on the west. Mama used to say it was the best of both worlds, with the village at their front door and the country out their back windows.

The path to the privy took Hattie around the cabin, past the smokehouse, the woodshed, and the freshly turned garden. Dew tickled and squished between Hattie's toes. She tucked eggs into her apron pocket and turned the hens into the chicken yard with Hambone and her nine piglets. Poppa had already filled Hambone's trough. The little pigs were eating, too. The smallest of the litter, Wee Willie, saw Hattie and came running.

He chased the cracked corn she threw to the chickens and got underfoot and made a general nuisance of himself. Hattie climbed back over the fence. She saw Dora June and her pa riding south from Johnson's Grove. She raced around to the front yard just as Constable Carlson turned the corner into Mount Hope. He stopped his horse at the front gate and called to Hattie.

"Is your pa around?"

"He's in the barn," said Hattie. "Climb down, Dora June."

"Can I, Pa?" asked Dora June.

"I reckon. But don't wander off, this won't take long." Mr. Carlson shifted his cud of tobacco from one long-whiskered jaw to the other and swung down after Dora June. He looped his sweaty horse to the fence that enclosed Hattie's yard and made for the barn on a choppy stride.

"We had riders in the night, lookin' for runaways," whispered Dora June.

Hattie's heart jumped. "Slave hunters? Did they find them?"

"Shh!" Dora June flung a look after her father. "Pa doesn't know I was listening."

"Did they find them?"

"Not yet. The slave hunters ate breakfast with us. They're plumb wore out from ridin' all night," said Dora June.

"They're staying with you?"

Dora June's pale, wind-torn hair fell in her eyes as she nodded. "For now, anyway. Pa's putting together a search party to help 'em find the runaways. He has to, it's his job," she added.

Illinois was a free state. But powerful pro-slavery men had hollered so about runaways escaping north that a while back, a law had passed that allowed slave hunters to search for runaways in free states, too. Poppa said it was an unjust law. It would do no good to tell Dora June. Already, she had her chin in the air the way she did each time they got close to that thin-ice subject.

"We passed Miss Garnet comin'." Dora June turned toward the road and added, "See? She's wearing blue today."

Hattie watched the schoolmarm, Miss Garnet, trek up the road and into Mount Hope. She was staying the week on the Jenningses' farm several miles north of Mount Hope. Her snug-fitting jacket and skirt matched her blue eyes. Wisps of golden curls and a poke bonnet framed her face.

"Do you want some walk-along company?" Dora June called to her.

"Not this morning, Dora June," replied Miss Garnet, touching the white frills at her throat. "I have papers to mark and some sweeping up to do."

"Teachers have to sweep up?" Dora June sighed as Miss Garnet went on her way. "And here I was set on bein' one."

"Me, too." Hattie twisted a dandelion stem, making

a ring for her finger. "Isn't she just the prettiest lady you ever did see?"

"Stylish, too," said Dora June. "See how her skirt poufs in back? You reckon it's all her?"

"I don't know. She's trim everywhere else."

"Puts a swing-swang to her walk." Dora June swung forward, hands tilted, fingers fluttering like little chicks. "Swing-swang, swing-swang," she chanted. "Swing-swang with me, Hattie!"

Hattie linked arms with Dora June. They circled the house, bottoms wagging, then collapsed giggling in the grass. Raised voices brought Hattie to her feet again.

"How'd you like it if somebody made off with your horses and you had no way of working your fields?" demanded Constable Carlson, a hitch in his stride as he bolted out of the barn after Poppa.

"It isn't the same thing," said Poppa.

"Shore it is. Property's property. You buy it, you don't want it stolen away."

"Property *is* property," agreed Poppa. "People aren't."

"I ain't goin' to argie with you. The law compels you to help me look."

"I answer to a higher law, Mr. Carlson."

"That's your last word?"

Poppa's long jaw hardened like a sunbaked brick.

Mr. Carlson jerked his hand at Dora June from

the other side of the fence. She darted off and out the gate and up behind him without a word to Hattie.

"If I catch wind you know more than you're ownin' up to, I'll be back. I'll go the whole hog, searching this place." Short in the saddle and stout as a stump, Mr. Carlson shifted his dancing horse and spat on the ground.

Chewed tobacco splatted at Poppa's feet. Poppa didn't budge. His gaze never faltered. But his color flared the way wood dust will when flung on hot coals.

Chapter Two

Hattie raced up the path between foot-high hollyhocks and over the threshold to Mama as Dora June and the constable rode away. "Mr. Carlson's got slave hunters at his house!"

A muscle jumped on Mama's scarred cheek. "Where's Poppa?"

"He's coming. Mr. Carlson's mad because Poppa won't help him look."

Hattie turned in the door with Mama to see Poppa fling his hat down at the washing stump in the yard. He stooped over the water basin. A sweat indention encircled his head like a wet halo. Hattie fancied she heard water sizzle as it hit his flushed face. She tucked fidgety hands in her apron pocket and flinched. "Oops."

Lines jerked at Mama's mouth like twiggy branches. "Where's my eggs?" she asked.

Hattie ducked her head. "Dora June and me got to playing and rolling in the grass."

"With eggs in your pocket?"

"I forgot."

"You've got the memory of a gallinipper!" Mama tugged at Hattie's apron strings. "Give me your apron, I'll see what I can salvage. Go wash your hands. Go on!"

Poppa was humming a single note as he passed

Hattie in the yard. It stuck in her head like the hiss of a steam whistle. She scrubbed her hands and face, then passed once more beneath the sweetbrier twining over the door.

Poppa had brought the climbing rose with him from his boyhood home in Rhode Island. That was fifteen years ago. He and the others in the Providence Farmers' and Mechanics' Emigrating Society believed they could make New England bloom on the prairie. They dreamed of New England-like farms surrounding a New England-like village where tradesman and churches and schools and libraries advanced New England virtues and values, among them a fierce love of liberty for all of God's children.

But as it turned out sweetbrier transplanted better on the prairie than some easterners. The land shifted from hand to hand over the years as some gave up and others moved on and newcomers took over. Now the countryside was being tamed by folks from hither and yon. Some, like Dora June's pa, believed the South had a right to her slaves. Others, Poppa said, while disapproving of slavery tolerated it out of fear that the South would pull out of the Union before she would give up her slaves.

Mama cooked the eggs Hattie had cracked in her pocket and brought them to the table with the porridge. Poppa stopped humming that one thin note and said grace.

By and by, Hattie stirred her courage. "What's Long Whiskers mean, he'll go whole hog, searching? Why would he search here?"

"That's Mr. Carlson to you, Hattie," said Mama.

"Mr. Carlson never had slaves," ventured Hattie. "Dora June said so. She says he's just doing his job."

"A man picks his job according to his thinking," said Mama. "The constable's southern born."

"But this is his home now," said Hattie.

"Yes, well, it takes all sorts to settle a prairie," said Mama. "Finish your breakfast, and I'll braid your hair for school."

Hattie bit into a piece of eggshell, finishing her eggs. It gouged her cheek and gum. She spit it out. But it was harder to rid herself of the gouge of words Poppa and her best friend's father had exchanged.

A few abandoned homes and outbuildings lay on the pathway to school. They were settling by degrees into the prairie from which they'd sprung. These remnants, along with the village square with its measuring rock, the cemetery, and the Congregational Church—now the school—was all that spared Mount Hope from being a town on paper only.

Last year a new village had been laid out beside the C & A Railroad, three miles to the west. *McLean*, they'd painted on the railroad depot. With the railroad there to make it grow, folks gave up on Mount Hope. The land on which the village was established had been sold. There was even talk of moving the church building into McLean. If they did, Hattie would have a long walk to school. Unless Poppa had his way about Kansas.

Miss Garnet was standing in the open door of the sturdy

frame building, a bell in hand. "Good morning, Hattie."

"Good morning, Miss Garnet." Hattie peered past her into the room lined in plank seats and plank desks. A center aisle led to the teaching platform and a podium. "Is Dora June here?"

Miss Garnet indicated the side yard.

Hattie's classmates milled beneath a spreading ash tree near the pony shed. Rowdy Jennings leaned against the tree, scratching scabs. He was the runt of the gathering. Recently, he had nearly died of smallpox, as his sister Maralee was fond of reminding everyone. He was flirting with death again, flicking a scab at J. B. North. Lucky for him, J. B. had his head turned and didn't notice. Dora June had her head turned, too, and her chin in the air. So did Tennessee Jones.

"I saw it with my own eyes," Tennessee declared.

"What'd you see?" asked Hattie.

"He heard the constable's looking for runaways, and next thing you know, he's seeing the Underground Railroad in his pa's straw stack," said J. B.

"I didn't say that a'tall!" argued Tennessee, his black eyes flashing. "Pa wouldn't go against the law that way. He says anybody that does deserves to be hanged."

"Is Mr. Carlson a hanging constable?" asked Rowdy.

"If he is, he hasn't hung anybody yet," replied Dora June.

Hattie stopped out of scab shot of Rowdy and asked, "What was it you saw in the straw stack, Tenny?"

"Somebody bedded down in it. The straw was all wallered down, and still warm."

J. B. snorted. "So he says, anyway."

"Yes, and I'll stand behind what I say!"

"You'll be standing behind pigs then, more'n likely."

"Do pigs pluck eggs out of a latched henhouse?"

"Your mama came up short on eggs?" asked Dora June.

"A lot short," said Tennessee.

"Did you tell Constable Carlson?" asked Maralee, twisting a red curl.

"Not yet."

"What's the matter?" asked Rowdy. "Are you scared?"

"Stay out of it, or I'll knock the scabs off you, Rowdy," warned Tennessee.

"If you suspicion runaways, Pa needs to hear it, Tenny," Dora June spoke up.

"What for? All they want is to follow the North Star to Canada and live free," said J. B.

"They'll freeze to death in Canada. If they don't starve first," said Tennessee. "They're better off with white folks to look after them. Anyway, Pa could go to jail if Mr. Carlson thought he was helping runaways."

"Mr. Carlson will have to turn up more than a little matted straw for evidence," reasoned J. B.

"We're missing a hen, too," said Tennessee.

"Reckon runaways stole it?" asked one of the smaller children.

Eyes widened. The circle tightened. Barking dogs came to remembrance. A shirt had disappeared from a clothesline. Milk cows had come home mysteriously dry.

Shadows had been spotted, melting into woodlands and down creek banks in the dead of night.

"I declare, would you listen to yourselves?" J. B. tossed his husky hands into the air. "All creation must be tramping through the neighborhood, helping themselves!"

Tennessee thrust his hooked nose in J. B.'s face and challenged, "You calling us liars?"

"What if I am?" countered J. B.

Taller, with eyes like wet stones, he pushed Tennessee out of his face. Their voices rose like gobbling turkeys. Fingers jabbed the air. Push came to shove. Hattie, Dora June, Maralee, and the others jumped back as the two boys flew at each other and tangled in the dirt. Their shouts brought Miss Garnet around the side of the building.

"Stop it, boys! This instant!" she demanded.

The boys rolled apart and came to their feet.

"What is this all about?"

Clench-fisted and red-faced, the boys traded blustery glares.

"Very well. We'll go inside and sort it out. Come along," said Miss Garnet.

Tennessee and J. B. fell in behind her. Once they'd circled to the front door, some of the children darted beneath the nearest open window so as not to miss an inch of Miss Garnet's going over. Dora June was edging off in the opposite direction.

"Dora June? I never did show you the baby pigs," Hattie called after her.

Dora June stopped and stirred dust with her toes.

Miss Garnet rang the bell out the open window. It clanged over the heads of the children flattened to the wall beneath the window. They jumped and scattered like shooflies. Maralee tripped over Rowdy and scrambled to her feet. One of his scabs was stuck to the back of her arm. She made a face and flicked it off. Hattie forgot her gougies and giggled. Dora June's mouth wiggled, too.

"They're the cutest little pigs you ever did see." Hattie pressed home her invitation. "Especially the runt, Wee Willie. The way he's eating, he isn't going to stay 'wee' for long. You can help me think of a new name. Can you come home with me for lunch?"

Dora June's smile faded. Her lip quivered. "I can't come to your house anymore. Pa says."

Chapter Three

Miss Garnet's school was a blab school. Some read aloud. Others spelled, ciphered, and recited out loud. In that din of noise, Hattie was a bird without a song. Dora June sat next to her, facing straight ahead. There was a shelf under each bench for slates and books and such. Hattie stooped to return her reader. Dora June did the same. But she wouldn't look Hattie's way.

A while later Hattie forgot and counted on her fingers right in front of Miss Garnet. Miss Garnet made her sit down on her hands. Dora June sneaked a glance. Hattie took a chance and waved.

"Both hands, Hattie," said Miss Garnet.

Hattie sat on both hands and moved her lips as if she were ciphering aloud with the rest of the children. She wasn't. She tangled her sums unless she used her fingers.

The morning passed, lump by lump. Miss Garnet dismissed them for lunch. Most of the children brought dinner pails and hung them from hickory pegs at the back of the room. Hattie tried to overtake Dora June. But Maralee got to Dora June first. They went out the door together, Maralee whispering in Dora June's ear. Trampling feet faded into the school yard. Hattie blinked her smarting eyes in the dim, quiet room.

"Did you bring a lunch today, Hattie?" asked Miss Garnet from her desk.

"No, Miss Garnet," said Hattie without turning. "Mama's expecting me home."

"You shouldn't keep her waiting, then."

Hattie's feet rang hollow on the wooden floor. She squinted in the noonday glare and angled for a sugar maple where Maralee and Dora June sat sharing lunches. Rowdy was sprawled on the ground between them.

"That's what I heard, anyway," said Maralee, passing Rowdy a jam biscuit.

"What'd you hear?" asked Hattie, stopping.

"That freckles are inherited," said Maralee.

"What's inherited?" asked Hattie.

"Means it's in the blood, passed on from your folks."

"My folks don't have freckles," reasoned Hattie.

Maralee sucked a strawberry as ripe red as her hair and replied, "Not on their skin, maybe."

"Where else would they be?"

"In the blood," replied Maralee.

"What good would freckles be in the blood? Nobody could see them," reasoned Hattie.

"Nobody wants to," said Rowdy.

Maralee snickered. Dora June kept her head down, picking black specks out of her cold corn biscuit, not saying a word.

Hattie scuffed home to Mama and broke down over Mr. Carlson getting in the way of her friendship with Dora June.

"There, there. He'll simmer down in a day or two and things will be back to normal," soothed Mama.

"But what if Dora June likes Maralee better than me?" sobbed Hattie.

"You go on being your sweet self, and you'll always have friends."

"Dora June, too?"

"Dora June likes sweetness the same as anyone else," said Mama.

If that was so, then why was she eating lunch with Maralee? Hattie mopped her eyes. She crossed to the looking glass to count her freckles while Mama put lunch on the table.

"Sun kisses," said Mama, looking on.

"The sun can kiss Maralee," said Hattie.

"I suppose it does with that red hair and fair skin," said Mama.

"It isn't leaving any marks. She doesn't have one freckle. Same with Dora June. Neither does Miss Garnet, and look how pretty she is."

"Be pretty on the inside where it counts."

"Can't I be pretty outside, too?"

"Freckles *are* pretty," protested Mama.

Hattie gave up counting. She had too many to count. Ugly, splotchy, awful things. "I wish they'd go away," she grumbled.

"They'll fade, come winter," said Mama.

"I mean *now*."

"Then wear your sunbonnet." Mama set a dish down with a clap that ended the conversation.

Hattie returned to school with her sunbonnet tied under her chin. She tied her manners down firmly, too, and was "her sweet self," all afternoon. But Dora June wouldn't even look her way.

When Miss Garnet dismissed them for the day, Hattie was first out the door. The children who rode horses to school let them graze on the village square in fair weather. One of the horses looked like Mr. Carlson's mare. It had not been there earlier when Hattie had returned from lunch. Was he sneaking around searching "whole hog"? What if he found matted straw the way Tenny had and made it out to be something it wasn't just because he was mad at Poppa?

Hattie raced her fears home. She heard Mama in the backyard. Hattie circled, heart at full gallop. "Is he here?" she whispered, looking about.

"Who?" asked Mama.

"Mr. Carlson!"

"Mr. Carlson?" Mama paused in taking clothes off the clothesline. "I haven't seen him since this morning. Why?"

Feeling foolish of a turn, Hattie shrugged and asked, "Where's Poppa?"

"Planting corn. He needs some help, so change your dress."

Hattie went inside. A chicken simmered in a deep round pot. She sniffed the stewy air as she changed her clothes, and wished that it was time to eat instead of time to plant corn.

Hattie strode into the yard just as Dora June,

Maralee, and Rowdy clopped by on Rowdy's old sway-backed mare. Dora June was riding behind Maralee. Rowdy was in front.

"What about your horse, Dora June?" called Hattie, pointing toward the village green.

"That isn't her horse, it's her pa's and he's doing constable work," said Maralee.

"I was talking to Dora June," said Hattie.

"I know. But she can't talk to you because your pa won't help her pa look for slaves."

"Tennessee says he's an abolish-ist," Rowdy spoke up.

"Abolitionist," corrected Maralee.

"Abo-li-shun-*ist*," Rowdy strung it out. "That's what Tennessee says."

"You're going to get the scabs knocked off you, that's what Ten-nah-*see* says," Hattie retorted.

Maralee put an arm around Rowdy. "Smarty."

"You started it," said Hattie.

"It isn't Rowdy's fault. He almost died, you know."

"So?" said Hattie.

Mama came around the house, loaded down with clothes from the clothesline. She wasn't singing anymore. Rowdy whipped up the horse. Maralee didn't look back. Neither did Dora June. Hattie's eyes swam.

"Dora June won't talk to me."

"The rest of you were doing enough talking, she didn't need to," said Mama. "What's this about Mr. Carlson's horse?"

"She's on the square."

"The green? Why didn't you say so?" Mama took the clothes inside and returned in a hurry. "We'll detour on our way to the field," she said, and grabbed the garden hoe in passing.

The detour took them by the grassy square. Mr. Carlson's horse was still grazing. So was Tennessee's pony, Pal. Hattie told Mama about J. B. and Tennessee fighting and having to stay after school.

"You had sense to stay out of it, I hope?" said Mama.

"I was my sweet self, like you said. All day long."

"Remarking upon Rowdy's scabs fell a little short, I thought."

"Him and Maralee started it."

"So you said."

They cut through the cemetery on their way to the field. Mama touched the crying stones engraved with the Crosby name. There were three stones and three babies, all born too early to survive.

Hattie had quit praying for brothers and sisters. She was scared of losing Mama in childbirth the way Mama had lost her mother. Anyway, she had plenty of family close by. Hattie slipped her hand into Mama's.

"I'm lonesome for company, aren't you?"

"The boys were here just a week ago," said Mama, meaning her brothers.

"Just the *older* boys. Anyway, that doesn't count. They were working," said Hattie. Her uncles had moved a herd of Texas longhorns onto nearby unturned prairie to graze for the season. "I want to see Gram Julia and Grandfather and Pierce. I want to have a great big dinner and play games in the yard and . . ."

Mama squeezed her fingers in warning. Hattie stopped short. There, at the foot of Mrs. Carlson's tomb was Mr. Carlson, flat on his back, his arms outstretched. His hat covered his face. He lay so screaming still, it sucked the air from her lungs.

Chapter Four

Hattie backed away on twittery limbs. A twig snapped underfoot. Mr. Carlson sat up with a start.

Mama planted both hands on the hoe and watched him the way hawks will from lofty heights. "What brings you back to Mount Hope, Mr. Carlson?"

"Constable business." He bolted to his feet.

"Has your company left?" asked Mama.

"No, ma'am. They ain't found what they come for yet."

"It's a sorry way to make a living," said Mama.

"I'm only doing my job, ma'am."

"I wasn't talking about constabling, Mr. Carlson. I was talking about those birds of prey flew up here from Kentucky."

"I don't recollect mentionin' they were from Kentucky."

"Then I'm mistaken?"

Mr. Carlson twitched like a horse vexed by flies. He turned his pale eyes on Hattie without reply. "School out?" At her nod, he said, "I'll collect Dora June, then, and be on my way."

"She went with Maralee and Rowdy," offered Hattie.

Constable Carlson thrust his arms into his jacket and strode off.

"Where's he going?" asked Hattie.

"Looking for his horse, I suppose," replied Mama.

"But she's on the square."

"Apparently that isn't where he left her."

Hattie watched Mr. Carlson enter a nearby shed. "He put her in there? What for? There isn't a cloud in the sky."

"He didn't want her seen. For all the good it did him," said Mama.

Mr. Carlson came out of the shed and shaded his eyes, looking this way and that.

"Should we tell him where she is?" asked Hattie.

"He'll figure it out." Mama made for the field just beyond the cemetery.

The soil was shiny black. It had been plowed and harrowed and turned into furrows. Poppa crested the hill, making cross furrows with a horse-drawn diamond plow. A second horse and plow waited under a nearby tree. A seed pouch was in the fork of a tree.

"Wait here," said Mama. She started into the field. All at once she stopped. Turned. Looked toward the village square. Mr. Carlson was there, trying to catch his horse. Mama retraced her steps to Hattie's side.

"Let's fill Poppa's water jug first," she said.

The jug was made from a dried gourd. It had a little water in it. But Mama was set on making a job of it. They left the hoe and trudged back to the house. Mama went inside to check on the stewing chicken.

Mr. Carlson trotted past. He didn't see Hattie at the well filling the gourd with fresh water. He rose in the saddle on his stubby legs and looked from the house to the outbuildings and barn and back again.

Mama came out and caught him at it. She waited until he was lost in a valley in the road winding toward Mr. Moore's gristmill, then flew for the field. Poppa's old mare, Angel, was resting in the shade beside the other horse. Poppa was dropping corn in the fresh-turned soil. Mama walked along beside him, talking and gesturing toward the cemetery and the town square.

Poppa reached the end of the row where Hattie waited with the water gourd. "Poppa?" asked Hattie, as a bead of water trickled down his leathery neck. "Why do you suppose Mr. Carlson will talk to me, but he won't let Dora June?"

"We didn't come to talk, we came to work," said Mama.

Poppa gave Hattie the seed bag. She slung the strap over her shoulder and took the hoe from him, too. He returned to the field with his horse and plow. Hattie followed along behind him, dropping three kernels to a hill. Mama followed her with the second plow, stirring the soil so it covered the corn.

The shadows lengthened. Afternoon gave way to evening. Hattie's shoulders ached. Her hands were tender from swinging the hoe, and her feet hurt.

"That's it for today, Hattie. Thanks for your help," said Poppa at sunset.

Hattie returned to the house while Mama helped Poppa with evening chores. In stirring the stewing chicken, she discovered onions. *Whole* onions. Ick.

Mama usually chopped them as fine as ravelings.

Gram was the one you had to watch when it came to onions. She put whole onions in boiling pots, and didn't cut them at all. Hattie knew it was wishful thinking leading her to her room. Gram wasn't going to be there. And she wasn't.

"You didn't cut up the onions," said Hattie when Mama came in from the barn.

"I'm sorry, darlin'. It's been a busy day. I must have forgotten. Miss Garnet's coming on Saturday," Mama reminded as she reached for her apron. She always shined the house when it came their turn to board the teacher.

Cheered at the reminder, Hattie sang as she mixed lard and water and egg together, a dumpling mixture Mama called pot pie. She stirred in flour until the batter grew stiff, then rolled it out and cut it into squares. Mama boned the chicken and returned the meat to the pot. When it boiled, Hattie dropped in her dough pies.

Poppa set the table and said grace. Hattie picked the onions off her plate and saved them for Wee Willie. She didn't have far to take them. He was waiting for her when she opened the cabin door after dishes were done.

"Wee Willie!" She scooped him up and rubbed noses.

"He's rooted his way out," said Mama. "That pig's turning into a pest."

"Pet. She means pet," Hattie whispered in Wee Willie's ear.

Wee Willie smacked and gobbled and made short work of the onions. Hattie stretched out in the open door and cradled the little pig in her lap. Next to onions, what he liked best was to have his ears and belly scratched.

"You're an itchy pig. Itchy-kitchy-coo," crooned Hattie.

Behind her was the light of the fireplace, the whisper of Mama's needle, and the creak of her rocking chair. Poppa read from the Bible. His voice ran rich and deep on themes of righteousness and justice.

Hattie's eyes grew heavy. The words ran together, a hum behind her sleepy thoughts. Her hands fell away from Wee Willie. The next thing she knew, Mama was on her feet, scolding.

"Shoo! Catch that pig! Thomas! Get him out of here!"

Wee Willie wiggled beneath Poppa's chair. Poppa reached. But Wee Willie slipped through his hands. Hattie stumbled to her feet.

"Stop, Wee Willie!" She chased him behind the spinning wheel.

But he darted between her feet and around and around a blanket chest at the end of Mama and Poppa's bed.

Poppa laughed as Hattie rolled to her feet, Wee Willie caught in her arms. Even Mama smiled. "He's a merry critter, I'll say that for him," she said.

"Rowdy, too!" Hattie blinked at sudden inspiration. A new name for Wee Willie, and a good one, too. She could hardly wait to let it slip at school.

Chapter Five

Hattie arrived on the playground the next morning to find Rowdy hanging by his knees from a tree branch, asking Tennessee about the slave hunters. Tennessee claimed he had seen them on his way to school.

"Did they talk to you?" asked Rowdy.

"No. But they tipped their hats as they passed. Beautiful animals they were riding," added Tennessee. "Fine glossy coats, flowing manes and tails and tall, too. Tallest horses I ever did see."

"What kind were they?" asked Rowdy.

"Tennessee walkers."

"Walkers? Why don't they get something that can run?"

"They *can* run," retorted Tennessee.

"Not as fast as Hasty, though," said Rowdy.

"That old nag you ride? They run a lot faster than that."

"Huh-uh," said Rowdy. "Nobody beats Hasty."

"Even Pal can beat Hasty, and he's long toothed as can be," said Tennessee.

"Mangy, too." Rowdy flicked a scab to the ground.

"He isn't either mangy! You're the mangy one." Tennessee dropped his head back, his black eyes snapping.

"I have a pet pig," inserted Hattie. She glanced

toward the pony shed where Maralee and some little girls were playing with hoops. "He's a fine pet. As *merry* as can be, running *merrily* over the yard."

"Your pa will butcher him, come fall."

"*Rowdy*, too," said Hattie, ignoring Tennessee's prediction.

Rowdy made a window in the branches. He bunched his scabby cheeks and pushed out his bottom lip. "What'd you say about me?"

"I didn't say anything about you. I said my runt pig is as rowdy and merry as can be. That's how I came to name him Rowdy Maralee."

Tennessee slapped his knee and laughed. "That's a good 'un, Hattie."

Rowdy dropped out of the tree, darted across the yard, and told Maralee. Maralee put her nose in the air and whispered something in Rowdy's ear. Rowdy broke into a big fat grin. He flapped his arms like a chicken and strutted across the school yard, screeching, "Hattie's gah-aught freck-gulls, Hattie's gah-aught freck-gulls!"

Hattie chased him around to the front of the building. Rowdy kept running. But Hattie stopped. Mr. Carlson was tying his horse to the fence. Dora June was with him.

"What is *he* doing here?" asked J. B. from the schoolhouse steps.

"Let's go see," said Hattie.

Mr. Carlson circled the building with Dora June at his heels. Hattie and J. B. caught up with them at the ash tree.

"Word is there's runaways hiding in the neighborhood," said Mr. Carlson as the school children gathered around him. "There's a handsome reward for 'em, so keep your eyes open."

"How handsome?" asked Tennessee.

"Read for yourself." Mr. Carlson took a handbill from his jacket pocket. He picked up a rock and tacked the paper to the trunk of the tree.

Tennessee and Maralee and the others crowded so close, Rowdy complained he couldn't see.

"Two men, a boy, and a woman goes by the name of Lizzy," Maralee read it for him. "Three hundred dollars for the woman and five hundred for the men."

Tennessee whistled. "Now *that* would buy a Tennessee walking horse."

"And then some." Mr. Carlson clapped Tenny on the shoulder. "You let me know if you see any sign of them and you just may be the lucky one to collect this here reward."

"That's blood money," said J. B.

"Oh? How's that?" challenged Mr. Carlson.

Miss Garnet rang the bell before Mr. Carlson could chew J. B. up like prairie hay.

The handbill was gone from the tree by lunchtime. Tennessee accused J. B. of taking it.

"Me?" said J. B. "You're the one wanting a Tennessee walking horse. What's the matter? Couldn't you memorize the descriptions?"

"Who needs to?" said Tennessee. "Don't any Negroes live around here."

"He's right. You mix pepper into salt and it shows up pretty good. Like freckles," added Maralee.

Rowdy guffawed and pointed at Hattie. Maralee smirked and whispered something in Dora June's ear.

"What'd she say?" demanded Hattie.

Dora June flushed to the tips of her ears and looked down at her shoes.

Hattie shoved past Rowdy. "If you were really my friend, you'd tell me."

"I can't. It was wicked."

"All I said was what happens when you mix salt and pepper," said Maralee with an injured sniff.

"That wasn't either what you said." Dora June turned and walked off.

"Well?" Maralee raced after her. "She started it, naming her pig after us. Dora June! Aren't you going to eat lunch with me?"

Hattie didn't wait to see. She'd had enough of Dora June and freckle talk and too much Maralee and Rowdy. If that wasn't bad enough, when she got home, Poppa came in from the field talking about Kansas Territory.

"Not *that* again!" said Mama, and the debate was on.

Pro and antislavery emigrants were pouring into Kansas to have a say in how it would enter the Union, slave or free. Poppa was itching to pull up stakes for the cause of a free Kansas. But Mama didn't want to go to Kansas and neither did Hattie.

The quarrel wore itself out over lunch. By and by, Poppa scraped back his chair, slipped his suspenders up to his shoulder, and picked up his hat of plaited rye. He stooped to whisker-tickle Hattie's cheek, then paused behind Mama's chair on his way around the table.

"I could use some help dropping corn this afternoon," he said finally.

Mama didn't answer one way or the other. But later, on the way back to school, Hattie looked back to see Mama, swinging her hoe, heading for the field. It would be the same with Kansas. If Poppa made up his mind to go, they'd go.

Chapter Six

Hattie trudged back to school and circled to the privy at the edge of the prairie. Maralee and Dora June had beat her to it. Hattie danced from foot to foot, waiting her turn.

"It doesn't have to be her parents," she heard Maralee say. "It's in the blood. That's what heredity is. Do you see now? I wasn't talking rough, I was just saying how heredity works."

"You mean it could be her grandparents?" asked Dora June.

Hattie stopped dancing and listened.

"But I know her Gram and Grandpa Tandy and they aren't . . ." began Dora June.

"Everybody knows Mister and Mrs. Tandy," interrupted Maralee. "But think, Dora June. It's Mr. Crosby always red-hot over freeing the slaves. Even if it means going against the law by refusing to help your pa look for runaways."

"I guess he is outside of the law, isn't he?"

"Looks that way," said Maralee. "Have you ever seen his ma and pa?"

"No," said Dora June.

"There you have it, then."

"Have what?"

"The reason Mr. Crosby won't help catch slaves," said Maralee with studied patience. "One of his folks has got colored blood."

Hattie drew her breath to deny it. But then they'd know she was listening. She pivoted, tramped to the woodpile, and rolled the biggest log she could find square in front of the privy door.

Her classmates were around front, except for J. B. and Tennessee. They saw her do it. But when Miss Garnet rang the bell, both boys trekked inside like they couldn't hear the girls pounding on the door and shouting to be let out.

"Rowdy? Where is your sister?" asked Miss Garnet.

Rowdy looked around, surprised.

"Dora June is missing, too. Go out and see if you can find them, please."

"Yes, ma'am."

"And tell them to hurry." With the blink of an eye and a faint frown, Miss Garnet quieted the low hum that went through the classroom.

Hattie folded her hands in her lap and kept her eyes straight ahead. They deserved it, both of them. She wasn't sorry. Not one wit. Though she *did* regret not getting a chance at the privy first.

Maralee flounced in, her face flushed and puckered and her hair standing up like the cockscomb on a Rhode Island Red. Rowdy followed with Dora June at his heels. Wilty and sweaty, she fixed her June-bug gaze on Hattie. Hattie tried to make her face as cold as Mama, staring down on the constable out at the cemetery yesterday.

Upon hearing what had kept the girls, Miss Garnet got behind the Sunday morning pulpit. She lectured on doing unto others as you wanted to be done and invited a confession. Hattie stared at a fly on the wall. The silence grew so deep, squirrels at play on the roof sounded like galloping ponies.

At length, Miss Garnet said, "There will be no spelling bee this week unless whoever is responsible for blocking the girls' privy door comes forward."

J. B. and Tennessee didn't appear to find that so punishing as to be tempted to snitch. Only the good spellers looked around in dwindling hope that the guilty party would come forward. Hattie copied their scowly looks so as not to stick out. Miss Garnet's eagle eye skimmed right over her.

"That's what she said, Mama. And Dora June believed her!" cried Hattie.

Mama dropped down on the washing stump, a bucket of freshly picked peas beside her. "And what did you say?"

"I didn't say anything."

"Good for you, darling," said Mama. She patted Hattie's knee. "Keep being your sweet self. This'll all blow over, you'll see."

Mama left Hattie to shell the peas and went out to the field to help Poppa. She must have told him about Maralee's lie. It wasn't mentioned over supper. But when the dishes were put away and Hattie was whispering her troubles to Rowdy Maralee, Poppa came out and sat down on the laundry bench beside her. He opened his Bible and read that life blood was precious to God. He said that it didn't matter what color it was wrapped in.

"There's no favoritism in God, that's what Poppa's saying," said Mama.

Rowdy Maralee oinked and rooted at Hattie's sleeve as she tried to weed out what Maralee had said. But words were like freckles—it took more than wishes to make them go away. She shifted Rowdy Maralee in her arms.

"Maralee says freckles are in the blood. Are they, Poppa?"

"I don't know. I do know you gave Maralee a hefty stick. Human nature being what it is, she's using it to lift herself above you."

Hattie stroked her piglet's curly tail, puzzling over Poppa's words. "How?"

"How does the slavocracy hold the Negro in bondage?" countered Poppa.

"They got the law on their side," said Hattie.

"And how did they get it?" asked Poppa.

Hattie thought it over a moment. "I guess there's more of them than there is of us."

"No, Hattie," said Poppa. "That isn't so. Those who actually own slaves are far outnumbered by those who don't. They hold their power the same way they gained it. They tickle the ears of their own race with thoughts and attitudes just like yours."

"Mine?" Hattie lifted her head. "What'd I do?"

"Let me ask you this," said Poppa. "If my mother or father came to America on a slave ship, would it change who I am?"

"You mean Maralee guessed right?"

"Would you love me any less?" pressed Poppa.

Hattie studied Poppa a long moment. His skin was ruddy. His hair was straight and reddish brown. His short whiskers, too. His nose was long and narrow. His eyes were blue and his chin was long and square.

"Would you still kiss me good-bye before school and race home later to help me in the field?" prompted Poppa. "Would you bring me water? If I cut my foot, would you wrap it for me? Could I lean on you until I got my strength back? Would you love me just the same, Hattie?"

"The same," she said.

"And yet you got your back up over Maralee's words. Now why is that, I wonder?"

"I can't help it, Poppa," said Hattie. "She's no better'n me and she's got no right to act like she is."

"No right, except the ground you gave up by your reaction," said Poppa. "By getting mad, it looks as if you're agreeing with her that it would be a bad thing to have black ancestors."

"I don't agree with her, Poppa," said Hattie quickly.

"That's good. Because it's a lie. Lies, like flawed attitudes, gain power in like company," Poppa continued. "Remember that, next time Maralee pulls your ear."

"She won't. She knows better," said Hattie. "Keep

your hands to yourself, that's Miss Garnet's all-the-time rule."

"And a good one," said Mama. "Why don't you put Wee Willie away now, before he roots a hole in your dress."

"He's not Wee Willie anymore. I changed his name to RM." Hattie caught herself just in time.

"That isn't a name, that's initials," said Mama.

"I know," said Hattie.

Maybe she'd fit Dora June in there somewhere, too. It would serve her right. Being her sweet self was a flat-out failure. Blocking Dora June and Maralee in the hot stinky privy hadn't worked, either. How could it, when they didn't know who had done it or why?

Next time, she would be more direct. She would plan better, too. She would get even away from school and away from home, where there'd be no pesky consequences.

Chapter Seven

Hattie did her chores at first light the next morning. She was filling her apron pockets with little green apples when a splintery branch toppled her into the chicken yard. Past experience had taught Hattie to take a fall relaxed and rolling. She rolled right over Rowdy Maralee Dora June. He darted squealing to his mother's side. The sour old sow struggled out of the mud and swung around, grunting threats.

Hattie scrambled over the fence with more haste than care. She dived her hands into her apron pockets and found she had lost most of her ammunition. Mama circled the cabin before she could replenish her supply.

"So here you are. We're waiting breakfast, and Poppa with enough work to keep half a dozen men busy," scolded Mama.

"I'll be right there," promised Hattie. She scuttled over the split-rail fence into the yard and splashed her face and hands and skunky feet at the washing stump before scampering inside.

Poppa said grace.

Mama said, "What's that smell?"

"Sweetbrier?" said Hattie.

Mama wiggled her nose. "Is that you, Hattie? Go wash."

"I just did."

"Use soap this time," said Mama. "Outside. And get between your toes."

Hattie fetched a cake of lye soap and returned to the wash stump. This time, she scrubbed until she really *could* smell sweetbrier.

On her way back to the house, she shaded her eyes, looking north. She couldn't see Dora June's home for the belt of trees growing along the creek that powered the mill. But she *did* see a distant speck that *could* be Dora June or Maralee and Rowdy on their way to school. Or maybe all three.

Hattie poked her hand in her pocket. She counted nine marble-sized apples. If her aim was good, it should be enough.

By the time Hattie finished breakfast, the speck in the road had grown into a horse and rider. It was a boy. He sat the horse too tall for Rowdy and too slim and straight and smooth faced for old Long Whiskers. And his toes turned out. Her cousin Pierce straddled a horse that way. The distance between them shrank. Hattie waved and ran to meet him.

"Pierce Tandy! What're you doing here?" she cried.

"Going to the mill for Father," said Pierce.

"The mill is the other way."

"I guess I know where it is. Where's Uncle Thomas?"

"In the field," said Hattie.

Pierce's tongue flicked to the corner of his mouth. He had a seed-sized mole there and the habit of worrying it at the least little thing.

"Something wrong?" asked Hattie.

"A dog jumped a rabbit right under Thorny's feet," said Pierce. "He bucked me off and the corn, too."

"Did the sack break?"

"No. But I can't hoist it by myself." Pierce prodded the mole again.

"I'll help you," said Hattie. "How far back did you lose it?"

"Couple of miles. But it's heavy. I'm not sure you can do it."

"Bet I can," said Hattie. She was eleven, the same as Pierce and nearly as strong. "Let's run tell Mama and we'll go."

Mama came out of the cabin, all smiles at the sight of Pierce. She asked after Gram Julia and Grandfather and Uncle Silas, Pierce's daddy.

Hattie used the wash stump for a mounting block and climbed up behind Pierce, impatient to be off. Mama kept talking. "It's clouding up, Mama."

"Gram said to tell you she's got a quilt ready to go into the frame," Pierce told Mama.

"When's she putting in?" asked Mama.

"Saturday, I think," said Pierce.

"Tell her to count us in. Hattie was just asking for a family get-together."

A raindrop hit Hattie on the nose as Pierce wheeled the horse out of the yard. "Let it rain, let it pour, no one cares but old Jake Moore," she sang.

"I care," said Pierce. "Father'll have my hide if that corn gets wet before I get it to the mill."

"Don't let it pour, don't let it rain! Wait'll Pierce gets home a-gain!"

"If the corn gets wet, maybe I'll just head west and keep going," said Pierce.

"You wouldn't say that if your poppa was talking about moving to Kansas," said Hattie.

"Sure, I would. I'd see what there was to see in Kansas and then I'd ride on to California and pan for gold." Pierce rubbed his lower back and asked, "What's that in your pocket?"

"Green apples," said Hattie.

Pierce twisted his neck around to look. "They're poking me. Get rid of them, would you?"

"I can't just yet, I'm going to need them here in a minute," said Hattie.

"What for?"

"For throwing, what else?"

"At who?"

"Dora June."

"Your best friend?"

"Not anymore," said Hattie. "Maralee Jennings made fun of me and told lies about Poppa, and Dora June went along with it. Here she comes, up the road." Hattie craned her neck, looking over Pierce's shoulder as they rocking along on Thorny. "Too bad Maralee and Rowdy's not with her, I'd settle her hash, too."

"You can't hit her from here," said Pierce.

Hattie flung a green apple just to prove him wrong. It fell so far short, Dora June didn't appear to notice she was under fire.

"Told you."

Hattie bristled at Pierce's smirky tone. "I suppose you think you can do better?"

"I could if I wanted to."

"Prove it," said Hattie.

"I'm not throwing apples at a girl."

"Why not? I'd do it for you."

"You wouldn't have to, I wouldn't ask," said Pierce.

"I'm helping you right now, aren't I?"

"You offered."

"All right then, if you won't help me, I'm not helping *you*. You can pick up your own sack of corn."

"Oh, hush and give me an apple." Pierce stopped the horse and twisted around, one hand cupped. "Give it here. Give 'em all to me."

Hattie emptied the apples into Pierce's hand. He kneed Thorny into a trot and flung the apples down.

"That's a dirty trick!" Hattie was about to climb down for them when Pierce reached back and squeezed her knee so tight, she couldn't wiggle free. She yelped until he let go. By then, it was too late for apple retrieving, and here they were almost upon Dora June.

Dora June had tried to pile her hair on her head the way Miss Garnet wore hers. It looked like a leaning shock of ripe oats. "She can hang up her fiddle, there isn't but one Miss Garnet," said Hattie as they passed.

Dora June walked on like she hadn't heard. Hattie swung around and looked back. There was something peculiar about Dora June from the back. It looked as if her shift was bunched up in her drawers beneath her skirt.

Hattie banged into Pierce when he stopped the horse unexpectedly. He turned Thorny around and called to Dora June, "How about helping us out? I lost a sack of corn about a mile up the road."

"Do I know you?" said Dora June.

Pierce's shoulders went up. "Pierce Tandy. Maybe you can hold Thorny steady while Hattie and I get the corn aboard."

"I'll help," said Dora. "Soon as Hattie says she's sorry."

"Me? What for?"

"For rolling that log in front of the privy door yesterday," said Dora June.

"That wasn't me," fibbed Hattie. "Why would you think it was me?"

"Because it *was* you. You don't have to lie about it. I'm not going to tell," said Dora June.

Hattie wiped a raindrop off her arm and jutted out her jaw. "If I say I'm sorry, will you take back what you said about Poppa being an outlaw?"

"I didn't say he was an outlaw, I said he was outside of the law for not helping Pa when Pa asked."

"Outside the law is the same as saying outlaw," said Hattie.

"I'm not goin' to argie about it," said Dora June. "The law's the law for the whole Union and it isn't right to go against the law."

"Well, Poppa says if the slaves aren't freed, there may not *be* a Union."

Pierce swung the horse around so sharply, Hattie

nearly fell off. "Hey!" she cried as they galloped away. "I wasn't done telling Dora June. . . ."

"Watch what you say," warned Pierce. "You'll get your father in trouble, talking like that."

"I wouldn't have talked to her at all if you hadn't of stopped," grumbled Hattie.

"I'm trying to tell you something if you'd just hush up and listen."

Stung, Hattie hushed. But Pierce had said all he had to say. He didn't let out another peep all the way to the spot where he had lost his sack of corn. The corn was heavy. It took everything in Hattie to lift her end over Thorny's rump and onto his back. She shook the needles out of her arms and prompted, "So *now* what do you say?"

"Thanks," said Pierce. He waved and rode off for the mill.

It was a long walk back to Mount Hope. Hattie was hot and grumpy and footsore by the time she reached the schoolhouse door. Her classmates were filing out for lunch. All but Dora June. She was up front, dripping tears on Miss Garnet's bottle green dress.

Chapter Eight

"You don't feel feverish, Dora June," said Miss Garnet. "Where does it hurt?"

"My stomach," whimpered Dora June.

"You've been weepy all morning. Has something upset you, dear?"

Dora June looked at Hattie. Miss Garnet's glance followed. Hattie shifted her feet, misgivings stirring like wiggletails over a stock trough.

"Why don't you stretch out on one of the benches and rest?" suggested Miss Garnet. "Hattie's here now. Would you sit with her, please, Hattie?"

Dora June lifted her wet June-bug eyes. "I don't want her sitting with me. She's mean."

"Me? You're the one who quit being friends."

"You quit, too," said Dora.

"You quit first!"

"Only because Pa said."

"You took up with Maralee like you didn't mind a bit. You let her talk about me and Poppa and I don't know what all."

Miss Garnet cleared her throat. "I hadn't realized . . ." She stopped and started again. "Did you eat before you came, Hattie? No? Then run home and eat. We'll talk more when you return."

Hattie hurried home and right into the middle of another argument. Sparks flew as Mama snatched the corn bread tin off the hearth and set it on the table.

"Those that have gone before? They've *gone* back east, Thomas. They've *gone* to California. I defy you to name one person who has gone from Mount Hope to Kansas Territory!"

"Could you discuss this with an open mind?" said Poppa.

"You leave doors standing open, varmints wander in," snapped Mama.

"Slavery is the varmint," replied Poppa. "Unless something is done soon, it will spread into Kansas and westward."

"You're one man."

"I have a vote."

"One vote. You'd uproot us from our home and my family for a single vote?"

"One vote cast at the right moment would have put Virginia on the road to freeing her slaves years ago," argued Poppa.

Mama's color rose, but her chin dropped. Her shoulders, too. "Sit down, Hattie. Your lunch is ready."

Hattie's face drifted toward the plate Mama put in front of her as Poppa asked the blessing. She didn't know any slaves. She had never even seen one. So why were their troubles causing quarrels at school and at home, too?

The forks chattered against the plates. Mama's scar stood out on her face like a twiggy branch as she tore bread and moved her jaws hard enough to chew leather. Hattie wasn't sorry to see the meal end.

She waited until Poppa left for the field, then escaped into the yard. RMDJ was rooting Mama's hollyhocks. Hattie scooped him up and carried him around back to play. Mama saw her there on her way to help Poppa in the field.

"I thought you left for school," said Mama.

"Can I stay home and help you and Poppa plant corn?"

"Not today," said Mama. "Go back to school."

Miss Garnet was watching for Hattie from the door. Her skirts swished as she led the way to the front of the empty classroom. Hattie tried to make her skirt whisper, too. But it was too limp.

"You and Dora June have been good friends for some time, haven't you, Hattie?" asked Miss Garnet, sitting on the bench beside her.

"We used to be," said Hattie.

"Dora June has given me her version of what happened. Correct me if I'm wrong, but it seems that inherited beliefs are at the bottom of your difficulties."

"In the blood, you mean?" said Hattie.

"Not exactly. What I'm trying to say is that your father and Dora's father have differing opinions. You girls are bringing those views to school and letting them come between you.

"I know there are things you and Dora June have in common," Miss Garnet continued when Hattie didn't venture a response. "Things you can share without danger of hurtful words and ornery attitudes arising. Why don't you build your friendship on these things?"

"I tried," said Hattie, scratching the welt of self-defense. "But Dora June's father said she couldn't play with me anymore."

"I can't promise you anything beyond this classroom," said Miss Garnet. "But I will tell Mr. Carlson that I am encouraging consideration for one another's feelings here at school. Perhaps he will see that it's unfair of him to ask Dora June to take up his quarrels. Nor does your father expect that of you. Does he, Hattie?"

"I guess not," said Hattie.

"You guess?"

"No, he doesn't."

"Good. Because all this bickering is counterproductive to learning. It is unpleasant, unnecessary, and, frankly, common."

Hattie had endured enough quarrels over Kansas to agree it was unpleasant. As for common, it had a different ring on Miss Garnet's tongue. Hattie brushed pig bristles off her skirt, saw dirt under her nails, and buried her hands in her lap.

Miss Garnet rose to retrieve her bell from the desk. Watching her cross to the window, Hattie yearned with a leap of heart to be softer, cleaner, and sweeter smelling. And in the future, she would talk only about nice things upon which people could agree.

Miss Garnet rang the bell. The children scuffed in. Dora June's dark gaze skipped over Hattie as she took her seat. Hattie started to smile, but her mouth muscles were stiff. Miss Garnet summoned them to the writing desk reserved for practicing penmanship. She gave them goose quills and sheets of foolscap. She had written in her neat hand a sentence at the top for them to copy.

A friend forgives at all times. Hattie wrote the assigned sentence. She sneaked a look at Dora June's paper. It was the same sentence.

A friend forgives at all times.

Hattie smiled first. Dora June smiled back. She dipped her quill in the ink pot and cupped one hand like a wall around the words she was writing. Then she turned the paper to Hattie again.

I have a secret. Let's talk at the measuring rock.

After school? wrote Hattie.

Dora June nodded.

Chapter Nine

After school Hattie put on her sunbonnet and walked with Dora June to the measuring rock. The men who had plotted the village had set the big stone on the village square to aid future surveying as the town grew. Children climbed on it. Roving livestock used it to scratch muddy hides. Bugs tunneled in its shade. But no one needed it for measuring, and now it was too late.

Dora climbed up on the rock. "Notice anything different?"

Hattie cocked her head as Dora June twirled. "You're lopsided."

"Am I?" Dora caught a handful of skirt and twisted, trying to see her own backside. "Hmm," she said, ducking behind the stone. "Close your eyes. Don't open them until I say."

When Dora June popped up again, she had a pouch in her hand. It was made out of corduroy, the same kind from which men's jeans were cut.

"It's a bustle," said Dora June, passing it to Hattie. "That's what Miss Garnet wears to make her skirt pouf out in back."

"Then it *isn't* all her? How did you find out?"

"Maralee. She snooped through Miss Garnet's things while she was sleeping."

"I guess you don't wear bustles under nightclothes?"

"Miss Garnet doesn't, anyway," said Dora June. "Maralee described it and I went home and stitched one up. It wasn't a bit of trouble."

Hattie turned the false bottom in her hand, seeing how it was made. "What's inside to make it puffy?

"Old rags. You got to walk careful, though, or it shifts out of place."

"I'll make one, too," said Hattie, returning the bustle. "If Mama will give me some rags."

"Doesn't have to be rags," said Dora June. "You could stuff it with feathers or wool. Even shelled corn would work. Though it'd be a mite lumpy to sit on."

"And it could sprout if you got the giggles and lost your water," said Hattie.

Dora June caught them, sure enough. So did Hattie. Like a breeze in a stuffy room, their laughter swept away lingering hurt.

"I'm sorry about this morning. And for blocking you in the privy yesterday," said Hattie as they started home.

"I'm sorry for hurting your feelin's," said Dora June. "I didn't mean to. But I didn't want to go against Pa, either. Then today after you went home, Miss Garnet said she'd explain it to him how she expected all of us to get along at school. So it isn't goin' behind his back, being friends. Not at school, anyway."

Hattie saw that Dora June was straddling a thin rail, trying to mind her pa and be friends, too. "So long as we're heart friends, I'll know you don't mean anything by it if you can't stop to play when your pa's around. You don't even have to wave."

"I'll pull my ear when we pass. That'll be the same as sayin' there's my friend Hattie," said Dora June, pulling her ear.

"I'll do the same, and that means I hear you, and you're my friend, too," said Hattie. She stopped on the path. "Pretend you're walking by with your pa, and we'll practice."

They were playing secret signal when Miss Garnet came along. She stopped and reminded Hattie to mention to her parents that she would be coming the day after tomorrow to stay the week.

"Can you go to Gram's with us on Saturday?" asked Hattie. "She's putting in."

"A quilting?" said Miss Garnet. "I'd love to. I'll stop today and tell your mother."

"She'd like that. We'll run ahead and tell her you're coming. Come on, Dora June," urged Hattie, catching her hand.

Dora June raced with her to the edge of the yard, then pulled free. Hattie didn't try to coax her inside. Instead, she tugged her left earlobe. Dora June tugged hers, too.

"I'll see you tomorrow. Don't forget to wear your you-know-what. I'll wear mine, too," Hattie whispered. She waved and turned and darted under the sweetbrier into the house. Mama was at the table rolling out noodles.

"Miss Garnet's coming."

Mama brushed the flour from her hands, changed her apron, and smoothed her hair. She met Miss Garnet at the door and invited her for supper.

"It's kind of you to ask. But Mrs. Jennings is expecting me," said Miss Garnet.

Mama sent Hattie to pick greens. Miss Garnet was gone by the time she returned to the cabin. As Mama washed the greens, Hattie told her about making up with Dora June.

"Didn't I tell you it would blow over if you gave it some time?" said Mama as they sat down to supper.

Maybe time was what she and Poppa needed, too.

Mama was quiet with Poppa and Poppa was careful with Mama. Hattie tried to think of something comical to help them to sweep away their noon argument with laughter the way she and Dora June had. Her efforts were disappointing.

But Poppa had smoothing-over ways, too. He helped Mama clean up the table and put the food away. He wasn't as thrifty as Mama and he didn't put the throwaways in the slop bucket. He used a spanking clean milk bucket. Mama didn't point it out or complain he was being wasteful. His help put her in a generous mood.

"Must be something in the ragbag I can spare," she offered when Hattie asked to practice her stitching. "Wipe off the table and we'll look."

"Shall I slop the pigs first?"

"I'll take care of it tonight," Poppa spoke up. He reached for his hat and left with the milk bucket.

Mama gave Hattie scraps from the sleeves of a dress Hattie had outgrown. It was indigo blue, a favorite color of Mama's. Hattie preferred sunny yellow herself. But bustles weren't for showing, so it really didn't matter. She busied herself with scissors, pins, thread, and needle.

"What are you making?" asked Mama.

Uncertain of Mama's view on bustles, Hattie played it safe and called it a pillow. The evening passed pleasantly. The bustle was ready for stuffing when Mama put her own sewing aside, returned her ragbag to the chest at the end of the corner bed, and bid Hattie good night.

Disappointed she hadn't finished, Hattie took her bustle to her room. She washed and slipped into her night shift and curled up beneath clean linen. Chirping crickets marked time as she fretted over her flat-as-a-stone bustle. She had promised Dora June. But how was she to sneak rags or wool stuffing from the next room without waking Mama and Poppa?

What about grass? The ropes creaked beneath the corn husk mattress as Hattie crawled across the bed to the window. The stars glittered like light through punched tin. She scrambled out over the windowsill and slipped in the glistening grass. Wet stuffing? What, then?

An owl flew from the barn as Hattie hugged herself, thinking. He dove for a patch of moonlit garden. A death squeak, and the owl lifted off, slapping the air with his heavy wings. He sailed over the straw pile, a mouse clutched in his talons.

Straw! Hattie shivered over the ticklish grass and

bypassed the dew-drenched straw pile. Set on dry stuffing, she swung the barn door wide. Pale lamplight brought her up short. Poppa never left lanterns burning. Who, then? The constable? His threat to search whole hog rushed over her. At night, while Poppa slept?

She was turning for the house to tell when shadows whispered in human voices.

Chapter Ten

Hattie's pulse reeled as a dark-skinned woman tipped over the milking stool, leaping out of the light. Mama swung around on an upside-down bucket, spilling needlework from her lap.

"Hattie! It's all right, Lizzy. It's just Hattie," cried Mama, relief in her voice and eyes and reaching hands.

The negro woman edged out of the darkness and righted the milking stool. She was older than Mama and ragged in a shapeless garment. A stained and faded head wrap covered her hair. Her shoulders were rounded. Her skin had a sheen to it. Her face was scarred, like knife prints left in chocolate icing. She picked up the quilt that had slid off her lap and brushed away the straw. It was the tulip quilt from Hattie's room.

"This is Lizzy, Hattie," Mama said, hands pressing her middle. "What're you doing out of bed?"

Hattie's gaze swung from the quilt to Lizzy and back to Mama. "I need straw for my pillow."

"You can get it tomorrow. Go on back to the house," said Mama.

Lizzy held the quilt out to Hattie. It was all coffins and crosses in the dingy light. Like Mr. Carlson, spread-eagled on his wife's grave. Hattie backed away.

Mama took the quilt from Lizzy. She draped it over

Hattie's shoulders and gave her a nudge. "Close the door on your way out."

Outside, Hattie looked toward the cemetery. Doves cooed from hiding places. *Or was it doves?* Her uncles made that same call, signaling one another while hunting in the woods. Hattie shrugged off the quilt, sped for the house, and collided with her father in the door.

"Is he watching?" she cried.

"Who?" asked Poppa.

"Mr. Carlson."

"He's getting some sleep," said Poppa. "Why aren't you?"

"I saw her in the barn."

Poppa didn't ask who. He didn't say anything at all.

"Hear that? There it is again?"

"It's doves," said Poppa.

"What if it's him, calling to the slave hunters to come and get her?"

"I told you—it's doves."

Tears filled Hattie's eyes. Her throat ached. Her trembling frame, too. "Why is she here?"

"We can't neglect what God has called precious."

It was too distant an explanation for a secret so close and large and dangerous. Hattie hugged herself. But the shaking wouldn't stop. The trembles were on the inside where arms wouldn't reach.

"Come along, and I'll tuck you in." Poppa took her by the hand.

"What about the others?" she whimpered. "Are they here, too?"

"No more questions, Hattie," said Poppa. "It's too dangerous."

Hattie cried and flung her arms around her father. He picked her up and carried her inside and to her bed. She clung to him, sobbing. "I don't want you to go to jail. Make her go, Poppa. Please make her go away b'fore Mr. Carlson finds her."

"Lizzy has thrown herself into God's hands," he said gently. "Can't you?"

God's hands seemed so far away! Poppa's were big and warm and rough and strong. At length, he uncurled her arms from around him, then stooped to kiss her forehead.

"Say your prayers now, and go to sleep."

Hattie heard him leave the house. She prayed. But not for sleep. For Poppa, watching out for Lizzy. And for Mama. She understood now why she was so curt with Mr. Carlson when they found him spying from the cemetery. And why she dashed to tell Poppa, then made a watering job out of it so it wouldn't look to Mr. Carlson like she was sounding the alarm. She understood, too, whole onions in the stew pot. *Lizzy put them there. She had been in the house, helping Mama.* Now she knew why Poppa had dumped leftovers in a clean milk bucket and taken it out himself. All that knowledge could be summed up in a word: abolitionist.

Aboli-shun-ist. Hattie strung it out in her head the way Rowdy had. The "shun" hissed in her ears. She'd been stung by it twice this week—once by Mr. Carlson in the barnyard. And again when Maralee made Poppa out to be an outlaw. But outlaws took for themselves. They did mean things and hurt people who got in their way. Even murdered sometimes. Poppa and Mama were trying to help, not hurt. So how was it that the law was against them?

After a while, there was sound in the next room. Mama opened Hattie's door and looked in. Hattie stirred to her elbow. "Did Poppa take her away?"

"You aren't to ask that, Hattie. You mustn't talk about it all. If people found out, it could cost Lizzy her life and go hard for Poppa."

"Is he home?"

Mama nodded. "You dropped your quilt."

"I don't want it anymore," said Hattie quickly.

Mama perched on the edge of the bed, the quilt in her lap. She traced the little ditches made by seams and highways of stitches. "Lizzy was injured, escaping," she murmured. "She had some of her children with her. They went on ahead while we nursed her back to health. Cold weather set in before she was well enough to travel."

Hattie turned her face to Mama. "She was here a whole winter?"

"We made a bed for her in the loft near the chimney." Mama stroked the quilt with work-worn fingers. "I lost the baby shortly after she came. She passed the time making the quilt top from the discarded clothes of her children."

"I should have guessed you didn't make it," said Hattie.

"Lizzy gave it to me as a memory quilt," said Mama. "The black is from a homemade dye she makes. The red represents birth."

"But the baby died."

"He died to this world, but he was born into eternal rest," said Mama. "Lizzy's people have no rest. Not this side of the grave, anyway."

Hattie's eyes swam as she peered at the ceiling looking for knotholes, like the one in her door. *Lizzy, unseen, but seeing their loss. Unheard, but hearing Mama cry over another lost baby.* Hattie brushed her neck. But the cold-hand feeling wouldn't go away.

Mama saw her shiver and covered her with the quilt. It held the weight of tombstones. Hattie pushed it away. "It's all coffins and crosses."

"There is no better symbol of love than the cross," reasoned Mama. "And symbols are the only language Lizzy has to mark down her thoughts. You remember, don't you, that it's against the law for slaves to learn reading and writing? Lizzy's speaking words of love and hope."

"With coffins?" said Hattie stubbornly.

"Tulips die back once they've bloomed. But come spring, they push up green shoots and bloom again," reminded Mama. "Don't you see, darling? Lizzy's using nature to remind us that God sent life to swallow up death."

The words seemed backward to Hattie. She rubbed her eyes, trying to erase the picture of little pine boxes going into holes in the ground. "I hate coffins," she muttered.

Tears glistened in Mama's eyes. But she patted Hattie's hands and hugged the quilt to her heart, murmuring, "Our babies are safe. They have gone ahead of us to where nothing can hurt them. That's what Lizzy's saying."

"What'd she come back for?"

"Because slavery is to her what those coffins are to you. She's showing her children the way to be free." Mama put her finger to her lips and added, "You musn't speak of this to anyone. Silence, Hattie. That's what Lizzy needs from you."

Mama took the quilt with her and closed the door.

Chapter Eleven

Nothing was said about Lizzy over breakfast. Slavery wasn't mentioned. Or quilts with hidden messages stitched in. Mr. Carlson or laws or outlaws or abolitionists, either. Just garden and corn and what was needed from the store. Poppa was planning to go to Atlanta tomorrow while Hattie and Mama were off quilting with Gram Julia.

Hattie arrived at school ahead of Dora June and ahead of the bell. Tennessee and Rowdy were on their knees beneath the ash tree. Hattie joined J. B. and a handful of classmates, watching the boys play marbles.

"Shoot b'fore Miss Garnet rings the bell," ordered Tennessee.

Rowdy took aim, fired, and missed. "Sun's in my eyes."

"Who's winning?" asked Hattie.

"Me," said Tenny.

J. B. scratched his back on the bark of the tree. "Rowdy would shoot straighter if he wasn't so busy making up stories."

"I'm not making it up," said Rowdy. "I saw it with her papers."

"Saw what?" asked Hattie.

"The handbill," said Rowdy. "Miss Garnet has it."

"It's a handsome reward for the one lucky enough to find them," said Tenny.

"How can she hunt slaves when she's here with us all day?" asked J. B.

"Maybe she isn't hunting them. Maybe she's hiding them."

"Where would she hide them? She's got no place of her own."

Hattie's secret burned like an iron as the boys guessed as to Miss Garnet's motives for taking down the handbill. She ducked her head, fearful the heat on the inside was working its way to her face. Maralee came along, rolling her hoop. J. B. stopped it with his foot.

"What did your folks say about Miss Garnet taking down the handbill?" he asked.

"They don't know, we didn't tell them," said Maralee.

"Here comes Dora June," said J. B., pushing away from the tree. "You aren't going to tell *her*, are you?"

"Well, no! She'd tell her pa for sure," said Maralee.

J. B. moved his foot as nice as could be, freeing Maralee's hoop. Maralee raced off to meet Dora June, rolling her hoop as she went. Her skirt poufed out in back. She twirled before Dora June like a redheaded top with a lop-sided bulge. *Crumb-de-dum!* Hattie turned her back so as not to be caught, green-eyed jealous.

But Dora June had already seen her. She came running. "Did you get your sewing done?"

"All but the stuffing. I'll finish it over lunch," Hattie said quickly.

Maralee sniffed. "If you have time. It takes a while to get it stuffed right."

"Hattie can do it. She's quick," said Dora June.

"I like sewing," said Hattie modestly.

"Not me," said Maralee. "It's boring and it tries my patience."

"Maybe your pa will buy you one of those newfangled sewing machines and make it go faster," suggested Dora June.

"Grandfather Tandy bought Gram Julia one. But Mama won't let me try it out. She's afraid I'll sew my fingers together." Hattie pressed her fingers together as if they had been seamed.

Dora June giggled and held Hattie's hand aloft. "Look, Maralee. Hattie's in stitches!"

Maralee yawned. Her funny bone wasn't nearly so ticklish over finger jokes as it had been over freckles.

The morning passed. Hattie went home, bolted down her lunch, and was on her way to the barn for straw when Mama sent her to the garden instead.

"But I want to stuff my pillow," complained Hattie .

"You can do that this evening," said Mama. "You don't want Miss Garnet thinking we keep a shoddy garden, do you?"

Hattie wondered how she could fret over that with so much bigger worries hiding in the barn. Or had Lizzy gone? Before returning to school, Hattie slipped around to the back of the barn where Mama couldn't see her. There was a loose vertical board midway along the back wall. A single wooden nail held it in place. Hattie pulled on the bottom of the board and turned it at the same time. The short plank pivoted on the nail, making an opening just big enough for her to slip through. She crawled on her knees, then stood up in Angel's vacant stall.

It smelled dank and dusty and of horse and hay. But all was quiet. So quiet, Hattie's heart sounded like hoofbeats. Was Lizzy here? Hattie heard something stir in the loft above her. She bolted back the way she had come and broke the bottom part of the board getting out. Mama called out the back window just as Hattie returned to the garden, and sent her off to school.

Dora June was waiting for her under the ash tree.

"I couldn't finish it, Mama wouldn't let me," said Hattie, before she could ask. "I'll wear it Monday. Where's Maralee?"

"In the privy, fixing hers. It keeps slipping."

Maralee came out of the privy and retrieved her hoop from Rowdy's unsuspecting hands.

"Hey!" yelped Rowdy. "I was playing with that!"

"It's mine. You can have a turn later," said Maralee.

"Yah? Well, your drawers are all bunched up," hollered Rowdy as she started away with her hoop.

Maralee flushed and plucked at her skirt and muttered at him to hush. He cupped his hands to his mouth and yelled even louder, "Look at Maralee! A critter crawled up under her skirt."

Maralee wheeled around and tore after him. Rowdy yelped and dodged and circled beneath the ash tree. He was gaining some when Tennessee stuck out his foot and tripped him. Rowdy careened into the trunk of the tree and curled up like a porcupine. Maralee jumped him from behind.

"I been sick, Maralee. I almost died!" he blubbered.

"You'll wish you had!" roared Maralee. She rolled him like a marble, pinned him to the ground, and lost her bustle in the tussle.

Children squealed and laughed, heaping coals on Maralee's fury. She grabbed her bustle and beat Rowdy over the head until the fabric gave. Feathers flew like January flurries.

"Chicken feathers! Why didn't I think of that?" cried Hattie.

"It's duck down," confided Dora June.

"Duck down?" J. B. laughed. "Duck down, Rowdy!"

"Duck! Duck! Duck down!" Tennessee took up the cry.

Miss Garnet swing-swanged around the schoolhouse, arm pumping. Maralee saw her coming and let Rowdy go. He staggered to his knees and blinked like a ruffled owl. He had feathers where scabs had been. In his hair, too. And under his dripping nose. They fluttered as he exhaled.

"What is this about? And what are all these feathers?" Miss Garnet's words popped like water in hot grease.

"It's Maralee," said Rowdy. "She had a duck up her knickers."

Miss Garnet caught Maralee before she could plow

the prairie with Rowdy again. "For-ev-er-more! Inside. Both of you."

Maralee and Rowdy brushed their clothes and followed Miss Garnet, heads hanging.

Dora June uncovered her pinched face. "Maybe I should . . ."

"You better," agreed Hattie.

Dora June slipped into the girls' privy while Hattie gathered feathers and the boys slapped backs and laughed. When Dora June returned, there was no sign of the bustle.

"What'd you do with it?" asked Hattie.

"I hid it in the weeds," whispered Dora June. Her mouth turned down at the corners. "Poor Maralee. I'd wring Rowdy's neck if he did that to me. Wasn't that just the awfullest?"

"Awful." Hattie blew dust from a feather. "Help me with these, would you?"

"What for? Maralee isn't going to want them, after that."

"No. But I do," said Hattie. She spread her apron on the ground. "Drop them right there and I'll tie them up tight."

Chapter Twelve

Maralee broke the record for tears spilled at Mount Hope school in a single afternoon. Her eyes were red and drippy when Miss Garnet dismissed them for the day. Hattie stuffed her rolled and tied apron into her bonnet and followed them out.

"Did Miss Garnet whip you?" Dora June whispered to Maralee.

"No."

"Then what are you crying about?" asked Hattie.

"If she figures out about the you-know-what, she'll tell Mama," whimpered Maralee.

"My bustle! I'll be right back." Dora June dashed off to get it.

Hattie swung her bonnet by the strings. "What'd Miss Garnet *think* you and Rowdy were fighting over?" she asked Maralee.

"I told her it was over the handbill."

"You didn't tell her you knew she took it, surely?"

"Of course not." Maralee looked back toward the open door and the children spilling out. "I told her Rowdy and me disagreed over Mr. Carlson's right to hang it there on account it's church property."

"Yes, and this church is against slavery, in case you don't know."

"Slavery, slavery. I'm sick of the word." Maralee kicked a stick that lay in their path.

Hattie swung around as Rowdy came up behind her, rolling Maralee's hoop.

"Out of the way, Freckles!" he hollered.

"He's got your hoop," said Hattie as Rowdy raced past.

Maralee sniffed and stopped at the gate to wait for Dora June. Hattie was about to walk on when she saw the constable riding toward the school. Tennessee saw him, too.

"Did you find those fugitives yet?" he called to the constable.

"Not yet, Tenny." Mr. Carlson dismounted and tied his horse to the fence. "I thought I'd ride over and see if you young 'uns have seen or heard anything."

"Nothing of any account," said Tenny.

"Dora June around?" asked Mr. Carlson.

"She's in back," said Maralee.

The constable swung in that direction, then stopped just short of the ash tree. "Say! What's become of my handbill?"

J. B. and Tenny looked at each other, then away.

"The wind, I guess," said J. B.

"What wind?" Mr. Carlson peered at J. B. through narrowed eyes. "Did you take it down, boy?"

"No, sir."

"It was me," Tennessee spoke up. "I took it. I can't very well find them without a description, can I?"

Mr. Carlson's scowl lifted. "Got your eye on that

reward, don't you, Tenny? Good, good! Sharp eyes. That's the kind of help I can use. I got some extree bills right here in my pocket. Tack it up for me, Tenny. Good afternoon, ma'am," he added, and tipped his hat as Miss Garnet circled the schoolhouse.

"Good afternoon," she replied, whisking the handbill from Tenny. "I'm sorry, Mr. Carlson, but I'll have to ask you not to hang handbills in the school yard."

"I'm just doing my job, ma'am."

"I know that, and while I commend your dedication to it, I have a duty to teach these children. How am I to do that when their minds are preoccupied with this sort of thing?" Miss Garnet asked.

Mr. Carlson shifted his chewing snuff to the other jaw and opened his mouth to speak. But before he got his words out, Dora June came along.

"Pa!" Her acorn eyes brightened.

Miss Garnet looked at Dora June the same way Mama looked at Hattie when she walked into the middle of a Kansas argument. A nerve ticked at the corner of her eye. "Run along home, children," she said, clapping her hands the way Mama did when shooing chickens from the yard. "Mr. Carlson? Would you join me inside, and we'll finish our chat."

Dora June walked to the village square with Hattie and Maralee, far enough to get her questions answered. Then she trotted back to wait for her father. Maralee cut through the tall grass to where Rowdy was climbing aboard Hasty. They passed Hattie on their way home. Maralee's hoop dangled from the saddle horn.

"Good-bye, Freckles!" hollered Rowdy, waving.

"Good-bye, Scabby," Hattie replied.

The dust had no more than settled when Long Whiskers and Dora June came along at a gallop. They went by before Hattie could get her hand to her ear. She gave her lonelies a shake and went inside. Mama was stirring soup in a kettle over the fire.

"Who was that, passing?" she asked as Hattie slumped into a chair.

"Mr. Carlson and Dora June. He came for her just as we were getting out."

Mama's head came up. "Where is he headed?"

"Home, I guess. That's the way they were riding, anyway."

"Good," said Mama. She sent Hattie to the field to help Poppa plant corn.

When it was time to quit, Poppa swung Hattie aboard Angel. Angel was sweaty and tired and hungry and thirsty and in a great big hurry for supper and her stall. Hattie couldn't hold her back. She squealed and bounced along as Angel galloped for the barn.

Mama's soup supper was tasty. There was no mention of Lizzy, Mr. Carlson, or Kansas. Then Mama put leftovers in the milk bucket and Hattie had the answer to the unvoiced question of Lizzy's whereabouts. She poked around and couldn't find the tulip quilt. Did Lizzy have it? Was she stitching more wordless messages into it? How long was she staying, anyway? Worries flocked like hungry mosquitoes.

Chapter Thirteen

"I'll be a while," Poppa told Mama, and took the bucket.

Mama left Hattie drying the dishes and followed him out. They stood by the wash stump, talking too low for Hattie to hear. After a moment, Poppa disappeared around the cabin on his way to the barn. Mama picked up her hoe and strode out of the yard.

"Can I walk with you, Mama?" Hattie called after her.

"I thought you wanted to stuff your pillow," Mama called back, strolling on alone toward the crying stones.

Hattie finished drying the dishes. She collected her bustle and her apron full of feathers and sat down in the backyard. Poppa was leading a team and wagon from the barn to the nearby straw stack.

"What are you making?" Poppa called to her.

"A pillow." Hattie trotted out to show him. "Where are you going with the straw?"

"It's for your grandfather," said Poppa.

"Are you taking it tonight?" asked Hattie.

"No. I'm sending it with you and Mama tomorrow."

Relieved he wasn't going anywhere, Hattie resisted asking what he planned to do about Lizzy and when and how, and who else was with her. She whipped the remaining seam shut with her needle, then tucked the bustle under the wagon seat for safekeeping.

RM had escaped the chicken yard again. He was rooting in the hollyhocks. Hattie chased him out and around back to Poppa's straw pile. When he tired of that game, she lifted him over the end gate of the wagon, climbed in after him, and stretched out in the straw.

Poppa's hay fork whispered from straw stack to wagon with a steady swishing stride. Hattie giggled as the straw fell over her. It was dusty sweet and scratchy and held the sun's warmth.

"Shh! Here comes your mama," warned Poppa.

Hattie heard the hushed laughter in his voice and lay still. So still she heard Mama's swishing skirts and the scratch of her hoe hitting the ground like a cane.

"Nothing's stirring that I can see," she said to Poppa. "Where's Hattie?"

Hattie burst to her feet with a whoop and a shower of straw. Mama leaped back, then laughed at herself and swatted Poppa, knowing he was behind Hattie's leap and scare game.

Poppa laughed, too. "Get down from there now and take your pig. You're making a mess of my straw."

Hattie giggled and climbed down. Mama kept Poppa company while she returned RM to the chicken yard. Once the wagon was full of straw, they all walked to the house together.

Hattie filled a basin with water, carried it to her room, and went back for soap and a washing cloth. Poppa was at the table with a lamp and a book. Mama was on her knees before the blanket chest at the end of her bed. There were no blankets, just her ragbag and clothing sent by women from Rhode Island. Hattie had asked Mama once why the women had sent the clothing. She had told her that they were for folks in hard circumstances.

Mama glanced up to find her watching. "I thought you were washing for bed."

Hattie swallowed her questions and retreated to her room. But she left the door open a crack. Sure enough, Mama left the house with clothes from the chest.

Hattie washed and put on her night shift. Poppa was still reading. He didn't even look up when she slipped out the door and sat on the stoop. Hattie hugged her knees and thought about Lizzy as night settled around her. It wasn't long before Mama came around the house on the path from the barn.

"I wish we could climb in the wagon and go right now to Grandfather's," said Hattie, making room on the stoop for Mama.

They'd done just that once on Christmas Eve, before the railroad tracks were laid. There had been snow on the ground. Poppa had pointed out the North Star, the one that had guided wise men and shepherds and kings. It had guided them to Grandfather's farm that night. J. B. said it guided runaway slaves, too, north to Canada.

Was that Lizzy's plan? Would she leave tonight and follow that star to freedom? Where had she gone when she left the shelter of their farm two years ago? Had she tried for Canada, and failed? Was she trying again? Was that what Mama had meant when she said that Lizzy was showing her children how to be free?

Hattie took her questions to bed.

The stars were fading from the sky when Mama shook Hattie awake. She dressed and braided her hair while Poppa brought the wagon around and put Mama's valise in the back. He caught Hattie by the shoulder before she could climb over the end gate.

"Ride up front and keep your mama company."

"Run and gather the eggs first, and we'll take them with us," said Mama. She gave Hattie a small straw-lined basket, adding, "Get the straw between them so they won't break. I forgot my sewing basket. I'll be right back, Thomas."

RM joined Hattie as she turned the chickens out of the coop and into the chicken yard. Hattie hooked her basket of eggs over one arm and picked him up. He wiggled and grunted and nuzzled her neck.

"Poor RM. You want to go, too, don't you? We'll ask Mama."

"Hurry up, Hattie. I'm ready to go," called Mama from the wagon.

Hattie dropped RM over the end gate with the basket of eggs and waited for someone to notice. Poppa was helping Mama up over the wheel and Mama was chattering last-minute reminders. Neither of them saw RM rooting into the straw. Hattie climbed the wheel and clambered up on the seat.

"Mama? Can I . . ."

"Hush darlin', I can't hear your poppa. What's that, Thomas?"

"I said tell the boys I'd welcome some help," repeated Poppa as Mama gathered the lines. "Whoever your father can spare."

"I'll ask," said Mama and called to the team.

Hattie couldn't see RM from the wagon seat in the dusky dawn. She didn't suppose Mama would turn back, once they got up the road. He was weaned, anyway. What harm was there in taking him?

Hattie sang to cover any piggy noise. Mama joined in. The sun rose as the horses plodded along. Hattie kept singing. She sang all the way to Johnson's Grove. Miss Garnet was waiting on the Jenningses' porch.

"What a lovely day for an outing. It's kind of you to include me, Mrs. Crosby," she called in her cheery voice.

Mr. Jennings came out on the porch, carrying Miss Garnet's valise. Mama had known him all of her life. He was her oldest brother's boyhood friend. "Howdy, Tee," she called to him.

"'Morning, Ellie." Mr. Jennings dropped Miss Garnet's valise over the side of the wagon and worked it down into the straw where it wouldn't bounce out.

Miss Garnet climbed up beside Mama and settled her skirts. Mama waved to Mrs. Jennings on the porch and smooched to the team. They lurched onto the rutted road. Hattie heard a muffled grunt and looked back. The bump had shaken the straw off RM.

Chapter Fourteen

Mama and Miss Garnet were so busy visiting, they didn't look back to see RM rooting in the straw. A bump in the road threw him off his feet. He grumbled and grunted. Hattie winced and tried not to look, for fear Mama would notice him and scold her in front of Miss Garnet.

The sun stretched and climbed the sky. Miss Garnet adjusted her bonnet. "Mrs. Jennings tells me that your father owns quite a lot of ground," she said to Mama.

"Father has made a little something for himself," said Mama modestly.

"I heard some grand stories about cattle drives."

Mama smiled. "From Tee, I suppose. He used to go along with Father and the boys." She waved away a pesky fly and added, "Times are changing, though. Father hopes to ship his livestock by rail next year, providing the new railway has everything in place."

At Miss Garnet's bidding, Mama went on to tell about her childhood on the prairie. Hattie loved Mama's stories. RM slipped her mind as Mama recounted big snows and Indian wars. She spoke, too, of the loss of her mother, and how her father remarried and Julia and her son Silas became part of the family.

Silas was Pierce's daddy and Hattie's favorite uncle.

Mama was fond of him, too. "He's doing a good job of raising his son. He takes after Julia in his nurturing, I guess."

"Silas is a widower?" asked Miss Garnet.

"No," said Mama.

"Auntie Crystal wasn't cut out for farming. So she took a train east and never even writes to ask about Pierce," said Hattie. "That's how come Uncle Silas and Pierce live at the farm. Right, Mama?"

Mama didn't answer. A horse-drawn peddler's wagon was approaching on the narrow trail. Mama was taking care with the team and didn't hear. Or if she did, she didn't waste breath telling how ex-Auntie Crystal went to court and untied the knot.

Miss Garnet didn't venture a comment.

The wagon seat was a mite unyielding. Hattie twitched and wiggled and in a moment of inspiration, snatched her bustle from beneath the seat and used it for a cushion.

McLean was the midway point between Mount Hope and Grandfather's house. Hammers rang from the store that was being built. There was a hotel now, too. A warehouse for grain and a railway station. The rest was still prairie.

The hotel keeper, Mr. Goodhue, saw Mama and hailed her with a sweep of his arm.

"Got something here for Mr. Crosby, ma'am." He stopped beside the wagon and withdrew a letter from his hat. He was also in charge of the local mail.

"Who is it from?" asked Mama.

"New England Aid Company, Lawrence, Kansas."

Mama's mouth twitched at the word Kansas and again when Mr. Goodhue named the amount of postage due. "You'll have to see Mr. Crosby about it. No hurry," she said, and bid him good day.

As they set off again, Hattie cast an eye toward the wagon bed. A pig ear showed out of the straw. But it wasn't moving. RM must be snoozing. Relieved, Hattie yawned and adjusted her cushion.

Mama turned onto a road that early settlers like Grandfather knew as the Chicago Trail. Once an Indian trail, the beaten path angled north across Illinois from Springfield to Bloomington to Lake Michigan's shores.

A gangly fellow on horseback was on the road ahead of them. His dark long-tailed coat and pants were wrinkled and his hat had more crimps than the stovepipe for which it was named.

Hattie saw his head bobbing. She giggled and sat upright. "Mr. Lincoln's riding in his sleep."

"My guess is he's reading," said Mama. She smiled. "I was a girl the first time I met Mr. Lincoln. I was staying a few days with my cousin Louisa, and we went to the store in New Salem where Mr. Lincoln was clerk. He had a book in his hand when we walked in. I reckon he had his thoughts on that book, for he overcharged Aunt Clarissa. Later, he realized his mistake and walked three miles out to the farm to return the difference. Word got around, and folks took to calling him 'Honest Abe.' The name has stuck to this day."

"Cousin Louisa has a boy the same age as me," Hattie spoke up.

"That's right. Louisa lives in Springfield now. Her husband's a banker, and a good friend of Mr. Lincoln's," said Mama.

"It's a wonder how he keeps that horse beneath him," said Miss Garnet, watching the horse and rider amble into the shadowy green timber. Mr. Lincoln disappeared from view, following the northbound road.

"He's going to court in Bloomington, I reckon," said Mama. "Mr. Lincoln is a circuit lawyer."

Hattie heard horses. She turned to see riders coming up fast. Mama gripped the lines tight and swung off the road. She headed the team east onto Grandfather's land. The wagon settled between the shady hardwoods of Funks Grove and a field of corn.

The horsemen followed. They thundered past, then wheeled their mounts around right in front of the wagon. Mama gathered in her startled team with a muttered exclamation. Hattie thought it was her high-spirited uncles teasing Mama.

But as the dust settled, it was strangers blocking the grassy lane. One was smooth-skinned and dimpled. The other was burly with a hawklike nose. Both men leaned forward and stroked the manes of their dancing horses.

Mama shot to her feet. "Move those horses! What do you mean, scaring my team?"

"I beg your pardon, ma'am," said the hawk-nosed fellow. "I'm Mr. Dungey and this is my associate, Mr. Hunnicutt." His gaze encompassed Miss Garnet as did the deep sweep of his wide-rimmed white hat.

A third rider galloped up, beard flowing. It was the constable. He stopped his wheezing horse alongside the wagon and tipped his hat to Mama. "These here gentlemen are from Kentucky, ma'am. They're looking for Negro fugitives."

"That's nothing to do with me!" said Mama.

"Begging your pardon, ma'am. But we have reason to believe the runaways may have concealed themselves in that straw you're hauling," said Mr. Dungey.

"Nonsense," countered Mama, color rising.

"All we're asking is that you let us do our duty and have a look."

"Do you have a search warrant?" asked Mama.

"That won't be necessary, surely," said Mr. Dungey.

"You cannot detain me without one," said Mama.

"I ain't certain about that," blustered Mr. Carlson.

"Mr. Lincoln is five minutes up the road," said Mama. "Go after him, Mr. Carlson, and we'll ask *him* how the law reads."

Hunnicutt rode to Miss Garnet's side of the wagon while Dungey conferred with Mr. Carlson. Mr. Carlson nodded and turned back the way they'd come.

"Is he going for Mr. Lincoln?" asked Mama.

"No, ma'am. He's going for a search warrant."

"Then we'll be on our way," said Mama. She sat down and urged the team ahead.

Hattie looked back to see the men following.

"Turn around, Hattie," Mama said sharply.

"Are we in trouble?" asked Miss Garnet.

"Not at all," replied Mama.

Hattie slapped her shoulder as if she were shooing flies and looked back in the wagon bed. The men's eyes were trained on the wagon bed. Hattie's jitters bit like horseflies. All at once, the straw moved.

Hunnicutt lunged forward on his horse, pistol drawn. Dungey snagged a whip from his belt.

Shouts and straw and singing whip collided with Mama's panther shriek as Hattie scrambled over the seat.

"RM! RM!" she wailed, and threw herself into the moving straw.

Chapter Fifteen

RM was stuck headfirst in the egg basket. He tunneled through the straw squealing and throwing his wicker-trapped head. Hattie caught his thrashing hind legs. She stumbled back to Mama and over the seat with the pig, basket and all.

Mama cranked her mouth tight as a bed rope.

"I was going to tell you," murmured Hattie.

"Sit!" Mama pushed Hattie down on her homemade cushion, picked up the lines, and set off again.

The men followed, eyes trained on the straw.

Hattie wrestled the egg-slick pig out of the basket. She wrestled sticky thoughts, too, weighing evidence. *The straw piled high. The north road. The look of horror on Mama's face as the men drew their weapons.* The wheels fairly creaked Lizzy's name.

Damp pressure built behind Hattie's eyes.

"Hush, Hattie," warned Mama.

Miss Garnet fished a hanky from her reticule. Its sweet scent mocked Hattie's eggy hands and piggy lap and her lawbreaking family. The 'shun' in abolitionist was about to sting Miss Garnet, too. Hattie mopped her eyes.

The trail hugged the curve between the woods and field.

Saddles creaked. Horses snuffled. The men were so

close, they would overrun the wagon should Mama stop
suddenly.

Grandfather's house came into view. It was two stories of stark white clapboard.

Gram Julia appeared in the open door. Her blue
dress and smile relieved the plainness of the house.

Grandfather strode out of the barn, gray-haired and
stout. His piercing gaze moved to the men. They slowed
their horses, giving Mama a little room.

"Who are these men, coming?" asked Grandfather.

"Slave hunters," replied Mama without expression.
"They want to look in the straw."

The twin grooves about Grandfather's mouth deepened. "And what do *you* want?"

"It's your straw now," said Mama. "It's up to you."

He glanced once more at the strangers, then helped
Miss Garnet down from the wagon. Mama handed down
her sewing basket, both valises, and climbed down over
the other wheel, unaided.

"Where are you going?" cried Hattie, clutching RM.

"To the house. Put that pig out of harm's way before
you come in," said Mama. She turned for the house,
Miss Garnet at her heels.

Pierce waved to Hattie from the pasture and loped
over to meet her.

Pierce climbed up beside Hattie. "Who's that?" he
asked.

"Slave hunters," whispered Hattie as Grandfather
strode to meet the men. "There's someone in the straw.
Don't look!"

Pierce corrected the impulse. His tongue flicked to the corner of his mouth. He lifted the lines and turned the team toward the barn.

Hattie blinked stinging eyes. "What'll we do?"

"Grandfather says unload it."

Mr. Dungey touched his finger to his hat and swung down off his horse. He offered his hand to Grandfather. Hunnicutt dismounted, too. He followed the wagon on foot while his companion spoke with Grandfather.

Pierce guided the team down the earthen path that cut through the dim, musky barn.

Hunnicutt fetched the hay fork.

Pierce vaulted over the seat into the back of the wagon and reached for the wooden fork.

"It's a hot morning," said Hunnicutt, withholding it. "I'll give you a hand."

Pierce's tongue moved over his mole again. But he took the handle above Hunnicutt's grip, saying, "Grandfather said for me to do it."

Taut skin creased as Hunnicutt squinted and set his jaw.

But Dungey strode into the barn and motioned for Hunnicutt to give Pierce the fork.

He did so. Both men moved to the end gate. Dungey crossed his arms. Hunnicutt spread his feet and watched Pierce from eyes cold as frosty stones.

Hattie hugged RM close and climbed from the wagon seat to the loft ladder.

Two of Mama's brothers, Uncle Pete and Uncle Cole, ambled into the barn.

Pierce glanced up. Something silent passed between him and his tall, young, prairie-tough uncles. He went back to forking straw, wisp by wisp, making a pile beside the wagon.

Uncle Pete slapped his dusty hat against his thigh, nodded at the men, and traded howdies. Uncle Cole eyed them without much interest. He leaned against a granary wall and spoke of crops and chores and horses and hunting.

Dungey shifted one foot and asked the nature of the hunt.

"Snipe," said Uncle Cole. "A little tame for you fellas, I reckon."

"Now, Cole," chided Uncle Pete. He angled the men an appeasing smile. "Don't pay him any mind. The neighbor boys beat him hands down bagging summer snipe last night and he's out of sorts, is all."

"Summer snipe?" echoed Hunnicutt.

Pete nodded and stroked his chin. "Winter ones are easier to track—snow and all. You boys get any snow down your way?"

Hattie wished Uncle Pete would keep away from them. There was something under their faces, something steel-edged. Surely Uncle Pete saw how intently they watched the dwindling pile of straw and knew that snipe wasn't these men's game.

Pierce had stayed to the edges of the wagon as long as he could. The straw was gone from the edges now. The middle was shrinking. Hattie's flinched with each thrust of the fork.

She retreated past stored grain cradles and reaping hooks and flails to the loft door. Holding RM back with her feet, Hattie swung it open just as Mr. Carlson rode up. He dismounted his lathered horse, hitched his trousers, and strode for the barn.

Grandfather scattered chickens coming across the barn lot. He clutched an ox whip in his knotty hand. Hattie grabbed RM. She raced back to the cutaway in the loft floor, dropped to her knees, and gaped as Grandfather stormed into the barn. He flicked his wrist, making the end of the rawhide whip twitch.

"You men go on and satisfy your curiosity and let these boys get back to work."

Dungey leaped into the wagon and took the hay fork. Hattie hid her face and covered her roaring ears as he drew back for the thrust. She didn't mean to scream. But when she opened her eyes, Grandfather stood below, looking up at her with that quick impatience he's passed on to Mama.

"Go on up to the house, Hattie," he said.

"My pig . . ." Hattie looked around for RM.

"The boys will see to him," said Grandfather.

She climbed down on trembling limbs.

Long Whiskers smoldered like a burning stump and muttered over wasted time.

Hattie cut a wide path around him and the slave hunters. She wasn't far from the house when RM came squealing after her.

Pierce scooped him up and handed him over.

"I thought I'd be sick," muttered Hattie, hugging RM tight.

Pierce's mouth tipped. "You didn't really think Aunt Ellie would have lead those fellas here if she had something to hide, surely."

"She couldn't help it! Those men overtook us, and . . ."

"Only because she meant for them to."

"She did not. That's crazy!"

"Where's your father?" asked Pierce.

"He couldn't come. He had stuff to do in town." Hattie stopped short. "You don't think he . . . But we've got the wagon, and, anyway, he was going south to Atlanta."

"South. The last place those fellas are going to look."

Hattie swung around to see the men striding toward their horses. Uncle Pete was with them.

"I wish he would keep away from them," said Hattie.

"Maybe he's inviting them to stay for the quilting bee."

Hattie didn't know how Pierce could joke. But if he was right about Mama playing decoy, someone should have told her. She clung to wiggly RM and shivered as the slave hunters ran their hands over the necks of their horses.

"Nice horses," said Pierce, watching them mount up. "Too uppity for plowing, though. They need their manes stroked just to get 'em trotting."

The men swung their horses around and headed north.

Pierce grinned. "See there? Aunt Ellie knew just what she was doing."

"But what if there had been runaways in the straw? What would Grandfather have done?"

"Hiding runaways is against the law," said Pierce.

"That isn't what I asked."

"You shouldn't ask what you asked."

Hattie glanced toward the barn and back to Pierce. "Does Grandfather know Poppa hides runaways?"

"Grandfather's a stockman," said Pierce. "Livestock is what interests him."

"That isn't what I asked. Does he? Tell me!"

"Can't. You talk too much."

"I do not!"

"Do, too."

Injured, Hattie jutted out her chin and kicked dust all the way to the house.

Chapter Sixteen

Gram was as cordial as could be to Miss Garnet. Hattie's aunts were, too. They had come from surrounding farms, eager to pass along news and recipes and quilt patterns. Child rearing, illnesses, home remedies, and new neighbors got covered, too. Their chatter soothed Hattie after the morning's rough start.

It was lunchtime in a whipstitch, then afternoon with time out for baby rocking and putting toddlers down for naps. The afternoon passed, and food was spread over the table again.

At supper Hattie's single uncles vied for the privilege of sitting next to Miss Garnet.

Miss Garnet didn't appear to notice. It must have discouraged them. When their plates were empty, they trooped off to the woods. All but Uncle Silas, and he had more sense than to hover over Miss Garnet like a fly needing swatting.

After dishes were done, Mama's married brothers loaded up their families and went home. The grown-ups retired to the parlor. Pierce had gone to the woods with the boys, so Hattie went to the parlor with Mama.

Miss Garnet spoke of her childhood home in Boston.

"Boston?" replied Uncle Silas. "I spent a year there once."

Was that the year he met and married ex-Auntie Crystal?

Miss Garnet's voice was low but crisp. It was that way in the classroom, too. Most of the time. Gram Julia had a gentle lilt to her voice. Mama spoke in a prairie drawl. Like Grandfather. Only without the rumble.

Hattie missed a few words. She was about to move closer. But Mama eyed her as if she was thinking about sending her to bed. So Hattie picked up scissors right quick and cut out quilt squares.

The light was poor. Her eyes got crampy and her fingers, too. She only meant to rest them a minute.

But the next thing she knew she was upstairs, and the sun was glowing pink through the curtains. Mama was gone from the bed, but Miss Garnet was still sleeping. Hattie eased out without waking her. She tiptoed to the window and looked out just as Grandfather strode out of the barn, thundering for the boys.

Frowzy-haired uncles spilled out the front door, pulling on hats and boots as they went. Grandfather swiveled and led them back to the barn. In less time than it took Hattie to shrug into her dress, Miss Garnet was up and at the window.

The yard was empty now except for Pierce. He stood like a leggy fawn with his nose to the wind. Hattie excused herself and flew down the stairs and out the door.

"What's wrong with Grandfather?"

Pierce swung around with a nervy twitch. "Somebody gave the horses haircuts."

"You mean . . ."

"Manes and tails clipped short as whiskers." Pierce shifted his feet. "Those slave hunters did it. Soreheads."

Yesterday came back in a rush. "The runaways. Is that what they're sore over?"

Pierce's gaze slid away. His tongue flicked over his mole.

"That's not it? What, Pierce? Tell me!"

"Pete told them we were going to the woods later, and to stop back by if they wanted some fun. So they met us after supper for some snipe hunting."

"What did you do? Outhunt them?"

"Something like that." Pierce edged away. "I've got chores. I'll see you later."

Grandfather's color was high when he came to the breakfast table, his eyes full of fire. Hattie's uncles scuffed in after him and took their places in silence. They kept their heads down and their mouths busy with food.

All except Uncle Silas. He made small talk. Gram Julia and Mama joined in, trying to gloss over Grandfather's temper storm. It was no small effort, what with the air so thick and snappy. Hattie drew patterns in the maple syrup left on her plate. She looked from uncle to silent uncle.

"What kind of a critter is a snipe, anyway?" she asked.

Their heads reared up as one.

"Snipe?" Grandfather cracked the word like a whip. His eyes flashed from son to son. "So that's it! You couldn't leave it alone, could you? Maybe you'd like to swat flies all summer. You'd be on the fitting end of the horse! The whole lot of you isn't worth one horsehair!"

"Is that jelly jar empty, Ellie? I'll get some more in the kitchen." Gram Julia scraped her chair back and fixed Grandfather with a calm and steady eye. "Gil, would you mind? It's one shelf out of reach for me."

"Let me," chimed Hattie's uncles over one another.

Pierce slid out of his chair and escaped with them to the kitchen.

Hattie followed. "What's he yelling at you for? It isn't your fault those men were bad sports."

Pierce's tongue darted to the corner of his mouth.

The others scowled and grumbled and muttered at her.

Bruised, Hattie wished breakfast and church were over and done with. For once, she had had enough of Mama's tinderbox family. She wanted Poppa. She wanted to be home.

It was a trying day that followed, the long ride home made longer by pecking anxieties. If Pierce was right, and Mama *had* led the constable on a goose chase so Poppa could see Lizzy on her way, then he could be in danger. Or had he successfully outfoxed the slave hunters?

Dusk was falling by the time Mama turned the team into the barnyard. Hattie scanned the empty yard. The house was dark. Her gaze lingered on the sweetbrier. The door opened beneath it. Poppa stepped out, milk bucket in hand.

Hattie scrambled over Miss Garnet's feet, and down. The shame of getting chased by slave hunters, the shock of shaved horses, the strain of Grandfather's tantrum, and the silent treatment from her uncles all fell away as Poppa set his bucket down and caught her in his arms.

"You're back!" she cried.

Poppa chuckled, his chin whiskers sticking to her hair. "It was you who left, remember?"

Hattie laughed and hugged him again. He picked up the bucket. They turned down the path, hand in hand. Poppa faltered a few strides short of the wagon and team.

"Ellie! What have you done to my horses?"

"There was a little incident at Father's," said Mama. "I'll do the milking if you want to see to the team. Leave that pig in the chicken yard, Hattie, and light a lamp for Miss Garnet, please."

Miss Garnet climbed down, gripped her valise, and set off for the house.

Hattie returned RM to the chicken yard, then raced inside and lit the way to her room.

"You want me to help you unpack?" she offered.

"That's kind of you, dear. But I can manage," said Miss Garnet. She took off her bonnet. "Perhaps your parents could use some help with the chores."

Hattie trekked out to the barn. Poppa lacked Grandfather's fiery temper. But he was careful with his horses. Especially in fly season. He patted poor old Angel's stubby mane.

"Gil has his hands full with those brothers of yours," he said to Mama.

Mama shifted on the milking stool. "Father didn't warm to their mischief much, I can tell you. I don't think the boys have heard the end of it yet."

"Why is Grandfather mad at them? They couldn't help it they were better hunters," said Hattie.

"A snipe hunt is a joke hunt, Hattie. A prank aimed at making a mockery of tenderfoots," said Poppa.

"How?" asked Hattie.

Poppa paused in measuring oats for the horses. "If we were going snipe hunting, I would give you a sack and a torch. I would tell you to wait while I beat the bushes and chased the snipe toward your sack."

"That's all I have to do? Hold the sack open?"

"That's what I would tell you," said Poppa. "Then I'd start back through the trees, whooping and hollering and shaking the bushes. By and by you would find yourself all alone in the woods with a burned-out torch and an empty poke."

"What about the snipe?"

"There aren't any snipe around here, Hattie. That's the point." Mama squirted milk at the growing puddle in the bucket. "The boys pull it on every greenhorn who comes along. I wish you should have seen their faces, Thomas, when Hattie piped up and gave them away."

"Grandfather didn't know?" Hattie clapped her

hand over her mouth. No wonder Pierce wouldn't talk to her!

Poppa's chuckle was hot noise in Hattie's ears. She kicked through the straw and out into the twilight and gathered a handful of stones. *Plip-punk, thunk,* they hit the gate.

Mama came along, milk bucket in hand. "Quit that, Hattie. Wash up and come set the table for supper."

Hattie washed. She was about to dash the water toward Mama's hollyhocks when Poppa cut across the yard. He plopped his hat on her head and held out his hands in invitation. Hattie splashed the basin of water over them.

"You aren't stewing over the boys, are you?"

"It's their own fault," grumbled Hattie. "They should have told me about snipe hunts. No one ever tells me anything."

"No real harm was done," soothed Poppa. "The boys will be laughing over it themselves once your grandfather cools off."

Hattie's thoughts shifted to other secrets far more dangerous. "Poppa? I thought there were runaways in the straw. I was scared we were going to get caught."

Poppa's gentle hand brushed her shoulder. "I'm sorry you were scared."

Hattie rubbed her burning eyes and whispered aloud the question in her head: "Where'd she go, Poppa?"

"You aren't to ask."

"I won't tell."

"Not on purpose, you wouldn't," said Poppa. "But

one innocent word to the wrong person could cost Lizzy her dream, maybe even her life."

You talk too much, Pierce's accusation echoed in Hattie's ears. Poppa must think so, too. She turned away, eyes smarting, and stumbled up the path toward firelight and blue-edged dishes waiting to be set on the table.

Chapter Seventeen

Uncle Pete and Uncle Cole arrived before school the next morning to help Poppa. Poppa hadn't expected both of them. He thanked them for coming. But Mama teased.

"Here I thought you were going to spend your summer being horses' tails."

Uncle Pete stroked his chin with a sheepish grin. "Mr. Lincoln stopped and had supper with us last night. He took Father's mind off the horses."

"And got him worked up over the political convention," chimed Uncle Cole.

"What convention?" asked Mama.

"There's going to be one in Bloomington at the end of the month," replied Uncle Pete. "The delegates are putting together a new political party for Illinois, one that won't talk out of both sides of its mouth."

"About slavery? An antislavery party?" Mama turned to Poppa. "You're going, aren't you, Thomas?"

"I'd be shirking my duty if I didn't," said Poppa. "Is Mr. Lincoln planning to speak?"

"He hasn't been asked," replied Uncle Pete.

"Whyever not? He's served in Congress and he's well respected. Maybe Father should put a bug in someone's ear," said Mama.

Poppa smiled at Mama's assumption that Grandfather's word carried that much weight. Uncle Cole tugged Hattie's braid. "Where's your teacher, Snipe?"

"Gone to school. It's our last week," said Hattie.

"What are Miss Garnet's plans then?" asked Uncle Pete.

"She's boarding with Tee Jennings's family for the summer," said Mama.

Uncle Cole tweaked Hattie's ear. "Come on, and I'll walk you to school, Snipe."

"Nobody's walking me to school. And you can quit calling me that!"

"Don't be stirring her up first thing in the morning, boys," said Mama. "Have you eaten? Sit down and eat again. I've got eggs coming out my ears."

Hattie made short work of her breakfast. She let herself out while her uncles were still eating. RM was rooting under the fence out front. He stayed underfoot all the way to the chicken yard.

Dora June came along as Hattie was finishing her chores. She laughed at the way RM tagged after Hattie.

"Is that your pet pig?"

"Yep." Hattie climbed over the fence. "I renamed him RM, but I'm thinking about changing it to Roam. It's got a proud sound, don't you think? The chicken yard can't hold him these days. See there?" she said, and laughed as RM wiggled under the fence. "He's a roaming kind of critter."

"I'd change it to Roma," said Dora June. "Look at him! Don't he look like a Roma? Aroma!" Dora

June bugged her eyes wide and laughed.

Hattie laughed, too. "It suits him, all right."

Dora June tickled Aroma's nose with a flower. He ate it, then wiggled beneath the split-rail fence closing in the yard and Mama's garden.

Hattie crawled over the fence and raced after him. "Mama will pickle your little roaming feet," she warned. "Help me, Dora June!"

Dora June joined the chase. A tangle of pea vines slowed Aroma down. Then he stopped for nature's call.

"Pee-hew! Aroma's aroma's a-roaming," said Dora June.

Hattie pinched her wrinkled nose shut and snorted and choked, giggling. Aroma cocked his head and snorted back at her.

Dora June fell in the grass, laughing. "Pa can keep his old hounds, I'm asking for a pet pig."

"I didn't know you had dogs," said Hattie.

"We don't yet. But we're getting some." Dora June wiped her eyes and brushed the grass from her skirt. "Mr. Dungey's giving them to us for putting him and Mr. Hunnicutt up at our house and feedin' them and all."

Hattie got a cobweb-in-the-face feeling at the mention of those two men. But it was so good to be friends again. She didn't want to start something.

Dora June waited on the split-rail fence while Hattie returned Aroma to the chicken yard. "You going to school now?"

"Soon as I tell Mama."

Hattie collected her sunbonnet and Mama's kiss.

Poppa, Uncle Cole, and Uncle Pete trailed her out the door.

"'Bye, Snipe," teased Uncle Cole.

"Be good for your teacher," said Uncle Pete.

"Who's that?" asked Dora June.

"Mama's brothers," said Hattie.

Dora June swung around for a second look. "Was it them took Mr. Hunnicutt and Mr. Dungey snipe hunting?"

"You know about that?" said Hattie, surprised.

"They told Pa about it. About the horses, too."

"They'd better look out. Grandfather doesn't like anybody messing with his horses."

"Pierce started it. He clipped their horses first."

"He did not!"

"He did, too," said Dora June. "He watched the horses while the men went hunting. When they got back to where they started, the horses were clipped and Pierce was gone."

"Well if he did, those men had it coming," said Hattie. "They stopped Mama on the road and blocked our way. When they finally let us go on, they followed us to Grandfather's house where they had no business."

Dora June didn't ask why the men had stopped them. Most likely, she had heard that from her father, too.

Their ease with one another popped like spit bubbles. Hattie caught herself humming the same note the way Poppa did.

Maralee and Rowdy came along on Hasty and offered Dora June a ride.

Dora June quit chewing her bonnet string and angled Hattie a sheep-eyed glance. "You want to?" she mumbled.

"Nope," said Hattie, tipping her chin.

Dora June hesitated about as long as it takes to blink, then clasped Maralee's reaching hand and pulled herself up behind her.

Hattie swung along with her shoulders set.

At the school yard, she looked back to see Rowdy ground-tying Hasty on the village square. Maralee and Dora June were picking wildflowers.

Hattie squashed a stink bug underfoot on her way to the ash tree. J. B. and Tennessee were squared off, arguing over the slave hunters. J. B. had seen them at a train station a few miles south in Atlanta the previous day.

"They couldn't get those horses loaded up fast enough," Hattie heard J. B. say.

"There's nothing funny about making an eyesore out of fine animals," retorted Tennessee. "Is it true your uncles took those men snipe hunting, Hattie?"

Rowdy bounded under the tree in time to catch the last couple of words. "Snipe? What's that?"

"It's a game bird," said Tennessee.

"Taste anything like duck?" asked Rowdy.

"Yes. But they're tricky to catch, on account they're nocturnal," said Tennessee.

"What's nocturtle?" asked Rowdy.

"Noc-TURN-al. Means they're active at night," said Tennessee. "The darker the night, the better the catch."

"Can I come with you next time you go?"

"I don't see how. The last I heard, Maralee doesn't let you out after dark," said Tennessee.

"Maralee isn't boss of me."

"He's right, you know. She isn't," J. B. spoke up. He draped an arm over Rowdy's shoulder. "What do you think, Tenny? Shall we cut him in?"

"I don't know. Maybe," grumbled Tennessee. "Sometime."

"I'll go whenever you want. Just let me know. I'll be there," cried Rowdy. He dashed toward the road, hollering, "Maralee! Guess what? I'm going hunting with the boys sometime."

"Maralee'll go and tell him, I suppose," said Tennessee.

"Maybe not," said J. B. "Could be she doesn't know."

Tennessee looked at J. B. His mouth wiggled at one end and his eyes got a spark. "We could ask her along."

"And let her hold the bag," said J. B., nodding.

The boys traded grins. Hattie grinned, too. J. B. and Tenny were on the same side for once. The side she was on. That and a patch of yellow violets almost made up for Dora June quitting her for Maralee halfway to school.

Hattie snapped up a handful of them. She dashed into the schoolhouse and gave them to Miss Garnet just ahead of Dora June and Maralee with their hands full of old wilty dandelions.

Chapter Eighteen

Beating Dora June to the punch made for a long day. Left to walk home alone, Hattie stayed after school instead and waited on Miss Garnet. She swept the floor, lined the benches on their marks, and wiped the slate board clean.

Miss Garnet looked up from her lesson book to see Hattie had finished. "Thank you, Hattie. You did a good job."

"Can you go home now?"

"Not yet, dear. But you may go. Tell your mother I'll be along in a while."

Disappointed, Hattie tied on her sunbonnet and ambled home to find Poppa at the edge of the field. He was passing coppers to the postman, Mr. Goodhue. Mr. Goodhue mounted up and rode away.

Poppa unfolded the sheet of blue foolscap. He read his letter, then called to Hattie's uncles who were working nearby.

"I'm going up to the house a minute. Hattie will bring you fresh water."

Hattie picked up the water gourd and hurried along behind him. "Who wrote you, Poppa?"

"A friend in Lawrence, Kansas," said Poppa. "The boys are hot. Don't keep them waiting, Hattie."

Hattie completed her chore, and started back to the house. She was at the gate when Poppa strode out the cabin door. He passed her humming a tuneless note.

Mama was at the hearth, punching the fire with the fire shovel. It spewed sparks and red embers. She scraped the glowing coals beneath the stew pot's iron legs. The popping clamor of iron, fire, and stone grated Hattie's ear. She edged over the threshold.

"What's wrong with Poppa?"

"He got a letter from a friend in Kansas," said Mama. "I need some onions. I'll be back in a minute."

Sparks skipped up the chimney at the whirl of long skirts. A cinder popped in the ear-ticking silence. Hattie saw Poppa's letter, spread open on the table. She checked the door, then crossed to the table and picked up the letter.

Dear Thomas,

It is because of your passion for justice that I write to you of the urgent situation in Kansas. You have only to look to the past election to see that the Free State party is out-numbered and outmaneuvered by pro-slavery factions. Now, Free State party leaders have been unjustly indicted for treason by the chief justice of the Territorial Court. I trust I am not imposing upon our friendship in appealing to you for help in this desperate situation. We need men of principle who will take a stand for Kansas being free for everyone. If we fail in this, we stand to lose Kansas Territory and the whole West to the slavocracy.

Footsteps sounded on the hard-packed yard. Hattie dropped the letter and jumped back from the table. Mama strode in with the onions. She left them unwashed on the table and stretched out on the bed without taking off her shoes.

"Are you sick, Mama?"

"My stomach is tipsy. I'll be fine in a minute." Mama closed her eyes and laced her fingers over her round middle.

It was a picture from the past, too deeply etched for mistaking. Hattie flinched. "Not another baby!"

Mama's eyes snapped open. Her face was all scar and red blotches. "Take those onions outside and wash them and don't be so brassy."

Schoolyard frets fled. Poppa's letter, too. Hattie grabbed the onions and stumbled out into the yard. Maybe she shouldn't have asked. But she had a right to know, didn't she? Who was it helped Mama stay off her feet the last time she was expecting?

Hattie jerked the tops off the onions. She poured water over them and more water, and peeled away the outer skins and kept peeling until they were shiny clean. Then she dried her eyes and went inside again.

Mama was sitting up on the side of the bed. "I'm sorry. I shouldn't have snapped at you."

Hattie's eyes blurred. "I guessed right?"

"Yes. It looks like we'll be getting a baby for Christmas." Mama patted the bed.

Hattie sat down beside. She looked at her shoes,

scuffed and dusty and water-spotted. "What's Poppa say?"

"I haven't told him yet," said Mama. "I don't think I will until after the convention. He'll get a clear picture of the situation in Kansas while he's there."

Bleeding Kansas, Hattie had heard it called. Gooseflesh prickled her arms. "I guess we can't go there now, can we?"

"We can't. But Poppa can."

"Without us?"

Mama sighed. "Try to understand, Hattie. They need men like Poppa if they are to turn the tide."

"We need him, too," said Hattie.

"We sure do," said Mama. "Especially now. I don't want to bury any more babies. I want *life* for this child." She studied her knotted hands and added softly, "But so does Lizzy."

"Is Lizzy having a baby?" asked Hattie.

"She's had many, all of them born into slavery."

"At least *she's* free."

"Is she, Hattie? With children still in slavery?"

Hattie picked at a wilty onion skin stuck to the back of her hand. "He'll stay home if you ask him to," she said at length.

"I know that," said Mama. "But slavery is bigger than just one baby. You know how it got started? Selfishness. Folks looking after themselves. Before long, they were building kingdoms on the blood of others. That's evil and it needs standing up to. That's what your poppa's doing."

"He doesn't have to go all the way to Kansas to do it, does he?"

"I hope not," said Mama. "But how can I stop him if he comes home from that convention feeling called to go? Would it be selfish to try? I don't know anymore. I just don't know."

Chapter Nineteen

The baby didn't seem real to Hattie. But then Negroes had once been a word without a face until she met Lizzy. Now they were as real as crying stones. As real as trouble reaching out by mail. As real as the cross and coffin quilt.

There were wrinkles at school as well. Dora June was cool toward Hattie, though not so cool as to attract Miss Garnet's displeasure. Hattie didn't want to disappoint Miss Garnet, either. She stayed clear of talk of slave hunters and horses with haircuts. By the last day of school, her peacekeeping efforts paid off. Rowdy, Maralee, and Dora June overtook her on her way home. Rowdy rocked forward on Hasty as if to hurry him along. "Get out of the road, Freckles," he hollered.

"Go around me, Scabby," retorted Hattie.

"Who's scabby? Not me." Rowdy showed off his scab-free face. "Scabs go away. Freckles don't."

"I don't care. I don't want them to go away," said Hattie.

"You're fibbing," said Rowdy.

"Huh-uh. They're sun kisses. Most kisses wash away. But not the sun's," said Hattie.

"Ble-e-e-c-k!" Rowdy squinted and pushed out tongue.

"You're safe," said Hattie. "The sun won't kiss just anybody."

Dora June grinned as if sharing in her joke. "So long, Hattie."

"So long." On impulse, Hattie added, "Come see me this summer."

Dora June didn't make any promises. But she tugged her ear as they passed.

Hattie tugged hers back, then turned to see Miss Garnet coming up the path. She stopped and waited for her teacher to catch up.

Miss Garnet smiled. "It must get lonesome for you once school is out what with no brothers or sisters to play with."

"I've got brothers. They just didn't stay to play," said Hattie.

Miss Garnet patted her shoulder. "Forgive me, Hattie. I wasn't thinking. You're right, of course."

They walked home hand in hand. Mama was tuckered out from helping Poppa in the field. Hattie fixed supper with Miss Garnet's help. It was a good supper, and a good-bye supper, too.

The next morning Miss Garnet left for Maralee and Rowdy's house to board for the summer.

The rains came, followed by warm sunny days. The corn sprouted and grew leaves. The weeds flourished, too. Poppa went from planting corn to plowing it. Hattie did her part, fighting weeds with a hoe.

By working from "can see" to "can't," Poppa kept up with the corn plowing as best he could.

It was drizzling the morning he left for the Bloomington Convention. Hattie watched from beneath the sweetbrier as Mama walked him to the gate. Poppa was taking straw to sell while he was in town. It was piled so high, she couldn't see Poppa as the wagon rolled away.

It drizzled again in the afternoon. The day was slow in passing. By evening Hattie was missing Poppa sorely. The cabin seemed empty without him in his chair reading or studying his map to Kansas Territory. Restless, she hung over Mama's shoulder, watching her seam triangles and squares, forming blocks for a new quilt. There was a lot of black in it. Surprised, Hattie asked, "Where'd you get black cloth?"

"I dyed it," said Mama. "You're between me and the light."

It wasn't even dark enough for fireflies when Mama pulled in the latchstring and told Hattie to get ready for bed. Hattie dreamed that Mr. Carlson's beard was coiled up like a scroll. She dreamed he unrolled it and caught Poppa's wagon that way frogs' tongues catch flies. She dreamed of quilts that rustled and hay that shuffled and of Mama's blue-edged dishes, talking in their sleep.

It was a restless sleep. Hattie awoke the next morning to find her chores already done and Mama looking yawny. It was that kind of day, cloudy and gray and cool. In the afternoon Mama sent Hattie to the garden. She was picking beans when Dora June came along.

Hattie jumped up so fast she spilled her pan of beans. "Dora June! How'd you get here?"

"Up the road and through the gate, same as always," said Dora June. Her acorn eyes twinkled as warmly as if they had never had trouble. "Do you need help, finishing the beans?"

"I'm finished, all but the snapping. Mama will do that when she's done napping."

"You wanna play school?" asked Dora June.

"Can I be Miss Garnet?" asked Hattie.

"I reckon. Where's Aroma? I can't be the only student," said Dora June. She turned a full circle, looking.

"In the chicken yard. Mud makes him lazy. Either that, or he's starting to understand he's a pig," said Hattie.

They crossed the fence that closed the yard in and stopped beside the second fence, the one that framed the chicken yard. Aroma blinked a sleepy eye at Hattie. But he saw she was empty-handed and couldn't be coaxed out of the mud hole. He was growing fast. So were his brothers and sisters.

A pink pig rubbed his hide on the trunk of the apple tree. He rubbed so hard, a green apple fell and hit him on the head. Dora June giggled. "He can be Rowdy, all scabby with mud. The red one can be Maralee."

"Who's going to be Tenny and J. B.?"

"There and there," said Dora June. "It's a big class, teacher."

Hattie giggled. "You can be teacher, too. We'll both be. Say we're twin Miss Garnets, all right?"

When Hattie tired of teaching mud hole scholars, she and Dora June climbed over the chicken yard fence and up the apple tree. The branches became a ship that rocked to and fro. It was a game Hattie had learned from Pierce, who yearned to see more of the world than the hind quarters of work horses.

Hattie heard rumbling in the distance. "Is that thunder?"

"It's stormy seas, remember?"

"No, really," said Hattie. "I hear something. Listen!"

Dora June cupped a hand to her ear, then made a window in the branches. "Shucks. It's Pa. I didn't think he would find me."

"You didn't tell him you were coming?"

"That would take the work out of it for the dogs," said Dora June.

"You got your dogs! Are they fun?"

Mama bolted around the cabin before Dora June could answer. She jerked the tulip quilt off the clothes-line, scurried past the smokehouse and the garden, and toward the back fence. Her day cap was sky goggle. Her thrashing skirts and panicky stride sent an uneasy ripple through Hattie.

"Mama? What's the matter?" she cried.

"Quick! Get down from there and run and tell Mister . . ." Mama saw Hattie wasn't alone and stopped short. "Dora June! Does your father know you're here?"

"He does now," said Dora June.

Hattie looked across the backyard to the wagon road. Mr. Carlson was coming, bringing two dogs on leashes. Or were the dogs bringing him? *Bloodhounds!* Their lusty baying went through Hattie like splinters.

Chapter Twenty

Mama grabbed a stout stick on her way by the woodpile, left the quilt there, and ran pell-mell for the front yard.

Hattie skinned her hands and knees, getting out of the tree and over two fences. She circled to the front of the cabin with Dora June at her heels. The dogs were at the gate. They leaped on hind legs, howling like demons and pawing the weathered boards.

"Stay back!" shrieked Mama. She beat the gate with her stick. "Get down! Get away! Pull them back, Mr. Carlson!"

Mr. Carlson was all sweat and lather, dragging the dogs back from the gate.

"It's all right, Miz Crosby. They won't hurt me," said Dora June.

Mama swung around. "They're tracking *you*? Child, don't you know they can tear you apart?"

"Aw now, Miz Crosby. Nobody's getting torn today." Mr. Carlson's beard rippled and his chest heaved as he got the dogs in check. "They got to be worked if I'm to do my job."

"You'll not work them on my property. Get them out of here!" Mama flung her pointing finger in the air as she said it.

"Ma'am . . ."

"The very idea!" fumed Mama. "The last I heard, we have rights even lawmen must observe. Or did slavery creep over the border while I had my head turned?"

"I guess we both know what's creeping over the border, and who it is showin' them the way," Mr. Carlson flared up like banked coals catching a draft. "Well, you can put the word out that these here dogs are about to chain Mount Hope's underground train to the rails!"

Hattie lost her breath as Mr. Carlson jerked his hand at Dora June.

Dora June scuttled over the fence and straight for the dogs. Mr. Carlson caught the leashes up short.

"Didn't I tell you plainly to stay away from here? What do you mean, going full chisel the other way?" he scolded Dora June as he wheeled the bloodhounds around. "What're you waiting for? Start walkin'!"

Dora June rubbed her ear as she set off with her father. But it looked more like distress than secret friendship. Hattie burst into tears. Mama dropped her stick and took her by both arms.

"Listen to me, Hattie! Are you listening? Run to Mr. North's and tell him I want four packages shipped."

Mr. North was J. B.'s father, a church deacon and a good friend of Poppa's. An *abolitionist* friend? Hattie's reeling thoughts froze in place.

"Mr. Carlson mustn't see you," Mama continued in the same low, urgent voice. "If you see anyone else, you're going to buy cherries. That's what you say if you're asked. Nothing more."

"Is it runaways?"

"It's Lizzy," said Mama. "You aren't to breathe her name. Packages. That's the word I want you to use."

"But I thought she was in—"

"Just go, Hattie. I'll explain later. That's my good girl. I'm counting on you." Mama relaxed her grip.

The North family lived more than mile away. There was no road. Just field and open prairie. When Hattie arrived, Mr. North wasn't there. Like Poppa, he had gone to the Bloomington Convention. Hattie delivered Mama's message to Mrs. North instead. She returned home with a basket of cherries.

Mama met her at the door. "Was he there?"

"No," said Hattie. "But Mrs. North was. She said J. B.'s brother will come for them. The married one. I forgot his name. She said look for him on the midnight train."

Relief eased the rigid lines framing Mama's mouth. "Good. Very good. Supper is ready. Wash up and we'll eat."

Mama had cooked smoked pork with the green beans Hattie had picked. There was wheat bread and wild strawberries, all in abundance. The cabin door was open to let out the heat and smoke of the cooking fire. Mama's gaze darted to the door at every sound.

"Is Grandfather home?" asked Hattie.

"He went to the convention. Why?"

"We could go there. The boys would know what to do."

"I know what to do. I just hope it's done in time," said Mama.

"Was Mr. Carlson snooping? Is that why he came?"

"At first, I thought so." Mama got up and closed

the door. "But when I realized it was Dora June the dogs had tracked, I got my wits together."

The confusion that had raced Hattie all the way to J. B.'s house and home again surfaced once more. "Didn't Lizzy like Canada?"

"She didn't go," said Mama. "She couldn't. Not with children still in slavery. She went back for more."

"Did she get them all this time?"

"No," said Mama. "You have no idea how difficult it is, Hattie. Over the years Lizzy has had thirteen children sold away from her. Some have changed masters over and again until she has lost track of them. Those whose whereabouts she knows are close to the plantation from which she fled. Two remain with her old master. There is no more dangerous place on earth for her, and yet she's determined to snatch them away to freedom. She's risking unspeakable horrors."

Lizzy's courage and the burden of secrecy settled heavily upon Hattie's shoulders. She thought fleetingly of the snipe hunt and her blunder. She wouldn't make that mistake again. She would guard Mama's confidences as if they were gold.

When the dishes were done, they went for a walk. Mama carried her hoe, alert for snakes as always. She had her eye out for snoops, too. Hattie could tell by the way she searched the cemetery grass. Intent on it, Mama forgot to touch the crying stones in passing.

Hattie peeked in the shed where Mr. Carlson had once left his horse. It was empty. So were the other abandoned buildings about the dwindled village. Everywhere, the dust and mildew and cobwebs appeared undisturbed.

Hattie climbed up on the measuring rock while Mama searched the tall grass of the village square. Wheat waved in the distance. Ankle-high corn fluttered. Birds sang as they came in off the fields, seeking twilight perches.

"Let's go back," said Mama.

They walked home under the dusky sky.

The cow was bawling to be milked. Hattie watched to see if Mama would take leftovers to the barn. But all she took was the empty milk bucket. The cabin was hollow and silent in her absence.

Hattie retreated to her bedroom and watched out the window. When Mama returned, she hung up the tulip quilt high in the window, safely out of reach of the low candle she left burning on the windowsill.

"Get ready for bed," said Mama. She gave Hattie a clean shift, then settled at the lamp-lit table with neddle and thread and fabric scraps.

Hattie amused herself with a small pile of quilt blocks Mama had pieced. The combination of brighter colors with the black was pleasing to the eye. She arranged the blocks so that black pieces came together and made a straight path across the table.

"It's railroad tracks. See, Mama?" she said,

"Sure enough," murmured Mama.

Hattie heard a soft sound. Soft as pebbles knocking together. Her pulse jumped.

"Go on to your room and close the door, Hattie. Quickly!" urged Mama.

Chapter Twenty-One

It was Lizzy and her sons.

Hattie watched through a knothole as Mama put out the lamp, then ushered them inside. The last of the four closed and bolted the door. He was young. They all were, except for Lizzy. The light from the low-burning embers showed wary faces. Fidgety hands. Long, muscular limbs.

"Did you rest?" Mama asked Lizzy.

"Until the dogs came," said Lizzy.

"It gave us a scare, too," said Mama. "Sit down while I dish you up some supper."

Lizzy followed her boys to the table. She studied the quilt squares Hattie had left behind and voiced her approval. "Jacob's Ladder. Good strong color, black. Says you're a safe house."

"I made my own dye," said Mama.

Hattie noticed Mama looked pleased with herself. You couldn't get black cloth in the store. You hardly ever saw it in quilts. But of course! That's what made black work as a secret signal. She watched Lizzy caress the cloth as she moved the quilt blocks to one side.

Mama put food on the table. The clatter of forks on plates muffled the soft conversation. The night was cool, the room drafty. Cold in her thin shift, Hattie felt her way to the bed and crawled under the covers to warm up. By and by, Mama slipped into her room.

"Is it time for J. B.'s brother?" whispered Hattie.

"Getting close." Mama retrieved the tulip quilt from the window and took it to Lizzy and her boys.

"I'll rest with you," Mama said when she returned. "Lizzy's saying good-bye to her boys."

"Are they going to take the quilt when they go?"

"I don't know why you worry over Lizzy's quilt," said Mama, settling beside her. "No one's making you sleep under it."

Mama didn't fear coffins and crosses. Lizzy didn't, either. Four of her sons were safe tonight because of the quilt. *Unless the constable came.*

Hattie rolled closer to Mama. "I wish Poppa was home."

"We'll remember him in our prayers," said Mama.

"Lizzy, too," said Hattie.

"And courage for her loved ones, far and near." Mama's hushed prairie drawl soothed Hattie's twitchy limbs. Her prayer grew softer and softer until it came from so great a distance, it got away from Hattie. Her eyelids drifted shut. She would rest a moment, and then she would look for Mama's slip-away voice.

Hattie dreamed of an owl that turned into a coffin and sat on the fence. When it grew arms and legs and started up the path toward the house, it frightened her awake. The sun was shining through the window and the cow was bawling again.

Where was Mama? Hattie stumbled up and into the main cabin. Mama was stretched out across the bed, still dressed, half covered with the tulip quilt. Hattie leaned closer.

"Mama?"

Mama's eyes opened with a jerk. Her hand went over her face, then down to her stomach.

"Did J. B.'s brother come?"

"Yes, darlin'."

"He took them?"

"All but Lizzy," said Mama.

"Is she still here?"

"No," said Mama. "Everything is fine. Go milk the cow while I fix us some breakfast."

Hattie went out to the barn. Poppa had taken the best horses, leaving Angel behind. She was almost as draggy-looking as Mama. Hattie knew without asking who had helped Lizzy on her way south to deliver more children to freedom.

Mama didn't eat much of the breakfast she fixed. Afterward, she crawled back in bed and didn't get up again until afternoon. Hattie was picking up wood chips around the chopping block when she heard Poppa's team coming. She dropped her apron full of chips and raced around front. His wagon rolled to a stop.

"Poppa's home!" she cried, and dashed out to meet him.

Poppa jumped down. He squatted and looked at something on the ground.

"I thought you'd never come home!" Hattie nearly

knocked him off balance, throwing her arms around him. "Lizzy was here. Mr. Carlson, too, with bloodhounds. She got away, though. Her boys, too. On account I went to Mr. North's."

"They weren't here at the same time," said Mama.

Hattie turned out of Poppa's arms to see her coming through the gate. "Can't you see you're giving Poppa a scare?"

"The constable came for Dora June. He didn't know they were here," Hattie amended.

"Whose wagon tracks?" Poppa indicated the wheel imprints in the soft earth.

"Mr. North's son boy helped us out," replied Mama. "Let's go inside. I'll fix you a bite to eat and tell you all about it."

Poppa took care of his wagon and team, then joined Hattie and Mama at the table. Mama untangled the sequence of events over an early supper.

"Lizzy saw her boys off, then we rode Angel into Atlanta and waited for the train," Mama drew her account to a close.

"She took the train?"

"I bought the ticket for her," said Mama. "It unnerved me a good bit. But not Lizzy. She didn't think she would attract much attention, so long as she was headed south."

"You did well, Ellie," said Poppa. He scraped his chair back. "You, too, Hattie. Now comes the hard part."

"Keeping what you know to yourself," said Mama.

"You must stop and think and pick your words carefully every time you open your mouth," cautioned Poppa.

"When I was a girl, children spoke only when spoken to," said Mama. "That took some of the hazard out of talking out of turn."

"My father belonged to that school of thought, too," said Poppa. He patted Hattie's shoulder. "I always thought it undemocratic."

Hattie pinched her mouth shut and started counting to herself just to see how long she could be quiet if she really tried. Poppa took advantage of her silence to tell Mama all about the Bloomington Convention. It sounded to Hattie a little like Miss Garnet's efforts for harmony at school. But in Bloomington, it was grown men coming together, trying to put aside differences for the common good. The common good, as Poppa described it, was to see Kansas enter the Union a free state, and not just for white men. He said it was the only way to keep slavery from spreading.

"That doesn't go far enough," said Mama.

Poppa agreed. "But I went knowing that moderates would be unwilling to demand slavery be abolished outright. Mr. Lincoln reasons we have to honor past agreements for the sake of the Union."

"Then Mr. Lincoln spoke?" said Mama.

"With the tongue of a moderate and the heart of an abolitionist." Poppa pushed his back and came to his feet as if propelled by some inner spark. "It was the most astounding thing, Ellie. He was both terrifying and beautiful."

"Mr. *Lincoln?*"

"I know," said Poppa. "He's homespun and he has a voice like a rusty hinge. But the other night, no one could match him. He spoke with power and authority. It was the end of the day. Suppertime. Yet no one left the hall. Newspapermen gathered from the state and beyond listened so spellbound, their pens lay silent."

"You don't mean—"

"Yes," said Poppa. "It was a speech to experience, a ninety-minute moment that went uncaptured in print. Oh, Ellie! How I wish you could have been there! It was like nothing I have ever seen.

"Time and again, Mr. Lincoln stirred us to our feet with his words. As we cheered, he would retreat to the back of the stage and begin again."

Poppa came out of his chair to demonstrate Mr. Lincoln's style. "'*We must make this nation a land of liberty in fact and not in name only!*'" he borrowed Mr. Lincoln's words. "And slowly, he would sweep forward again, driving home his point as he advanced. Growing larger before our eyes. Stretching into a towering, terrifying fury. And just when you were certain he could loom no taller, he would throw his arms in the air."

Hattie jumped as Poppa threw his arms with a roar:

"'*We say to our Southern brethern, we will* **not** *go out of the Union and you* **shan't!**'"

"What about Kansas?" asked Mama. "What did he say about Kansas?"

"Ah, Kansas." The animation drained from Poppa's face. His mouth turned grim. "Last week, troopers marched into Lawrence with warrants for the arrest of abolitionist leaders."

"You expected as much after the letter you received," said Mama.

"Yes," said Poppa. "But not the lawlessness that followed. Before the day was over, the Free-State Hotel was fired on by cannons and burned. Newspaper presses were destroyed. Stores and homes were pillaged and Governor Robinson's home went up in flames."

Hattie shivered and pressed closer to Mama. "You aren't going there, are you, Poppa?"

"Hush, Hattie," murmured Mama. To Poppa, she said, "What is being done to these lawbreakers?"

"They *were* the law, Ellie. A sheriff, and a United States marshal, with a militia for backup."

"Pro-slavery in sympathy?" At Poppa's terse nod, Mama shuddered. "What now?"

"Kansas must be free," said Poppa. "Even at great personal sacrifice."

"Mr. Lincoln said that?"

"No, Ellie. Those words are mine," said Poppa.

Mama's arm slipped away from Hattie. One hand pushed crumbs back from the table's edge. The other drifted to her stomach.

Fear gripped Hattie's heart. Vow of silence forgotten, she blurted, "Even if Mama has a baby?"

Chapter Twenty-Two

Mama sent Hattie outside. She wandered out to the chicken yard and watched Aroma root for grubs. Poppa found her there. Hattie braced herself and sneaked a glance. He didn't look cross. Just grave.

"It's hard work keeping a cabin and looking after a family," he said. "I want you to help your mama all you can."

"I will." Hattie rolled a flowering weed between her palms. "What about Kansas?"

"A man's family comes first."

Hattie felt as if the measuring rock had been rolled off her shoulders. Mama swung through the gate without looking in their direction. She took her hoe, leaning against the fence, and crossed the road.

Poppa shaded his eyes.

"What do you see?" asked Hattie.

"I'm watching the corn grow," he said.

But he wasn't. He was watching Mama swing along, angling for the crying stones. Hattie's palms were sticky with dandelion juice. She tossed the weed to Aroma and slipped her hand into Poppa's.

"Maybe it will be all right this time."

"Maybe," said Poppa.

Hattie took over the milking and the churning. She

helped with the washing and cooking, too. Sunshine and rain took turns nurturing the garden and Poppa's fields. They were flourishing.

The baby was growing, too. By midsummer Mama was filling out a loose-fitting dress. But there was no letup in work. The garden was producing more food than they could eat. It had to be harvested and kept for winter.

Hattie did the hoeing, the picking, the digging, and left the sit-down chores to Mama. Most of what was shelled and snapped and cleaned and sliced had to be dried in the sunshine before it could be stored away. Poppa helped, too, when he had the time.

"I'm fine. Just a little tired, is all," Mama said, every time he asked.

But despite efforts to lighten Mama's load, Mama had trouble in late September. One morning, she didn't get up. Dr. Proctor came and stayed late into the evening.

Poppa came out to the barn where Hattie had been sent to milk. His face was so long, Hattie burst into tears.

"Mama's going to be fine," Poppa said, and drew Hattie into his arms. "It was a girl. She had made the journey safely, but she couldn't stay. She just wasn't big enough to hold her own."

The stubble on Poppa's quivering chin snagged Hattie's hair. Together, they returned to the cabin. Mama lay on her side, cradling a blanket-wrapped bundle. The doctor reached over and arranged the blanket so that it covered the baby's face.

"Can I hold her?" whispered Hattie.

Mama lifted her gaze to Hattie. It was red rimmed and heavy and damp. Moist heat pressed at Hattie's eyelids. Blindly, she reached for the baby. Mama laid her in Hattie's arms. She weighed no more than a pair of goose eggs. Hattie folded back the blanket. Her heart jumped. The baby had not been bathed.

The doctor gathered his things. He warned Mama to get plenty of rest. When he had gone Poppa drew water from the fire kettle. He poured it into a china basin Mama saved for company.

"Take her to Poppa," said Mama.

Hattie carried her sister to Poppa. He took her in his arms and peeled away the blanket.

"She'll be pretty once we get her cleaned up. Roll up your sleeve. Put your elbow in the water."

The water felt too hot to Hattie. She cooled it with a dipper from the drinking bucket until it was just right. Poppa lowered the baby into the basin. He supported her head in one hand and her tiny body in the other.

"Wash her face first. Gently, Hattie," murmured Mama from the bed.

Hattie's fingers turned stiff and clumsy. She squeezed a little water over the baby's face, then patted her with the cloth.

"Rinse out your rag, that's it," said Poppa.

Hattie rubbed her sister's round cheeks clean. Her dimpled chin. Her mouth, tinged in blue. From the blood emerged a little creature with tiny fingers and a fuzz of red hair.

Hattie let go a breath of tearful wonder. "She's pretty. See, Mama, how pretty she is?" She carried the baby to Mama.

"She'd have had your freckles, with hair that red," said Mama.

Together, they dressed Hattie's little sister in a tiny pink gown that had once been Hattie's. Mama named her Louisa for her favorite cousin. Poppa worked into the night building a tiny coffin. The next day Mama sat in a chair beneath the sweetbrier, holding Hattie's hand as Poppa read the now familiar words about mortality being swallowed up by life. He buried Louisa out there among the crying stones. He didn't throw the dirt. He knelt with his shovel and dropped it gently, from his knees.

Later, when Mama was stronger, Gram and Grandfather and all of the family came. Poppa had been to town for a headstone. Cross shaped, it was engraved with Louisa's name. The grown-ups sang "Swing Low, Sweet Chariot." It made Hattie think about Lizzy gathering her children home. To them, freedom was a new life. Their bondage had been swallowed up by life. Louisa had life, too. Just not where they could hold her and sing a rock-a-bye song.

Chapter Twenty-Three

The apples ripened. Frost kissed the leaves. It sweetened the persimmons and glazed the countryside. School resumed, but Hattie couldn't go. Poppa was picking corn and Mama wasn't herself yet. She welcomed Hattie's helping hands and her hugs and chatter too.

Rowdy, Maralee, and Dora June came along on old Hasty on the first day of school. Rowdy was riding in front. He saw Hattie feeding the chickens and hollered, "Hey, Freckles! I'll race you to school."

"I can't today. I'm helping Mama," Hattie called back.

"With roundup?" hollered Rowdy.

"No. It isn't time yet."

"What, then?" asked Rowdy.

Maralee leaned forward and whispered in Rowdy's ear. He lifted his shoulder and grumbled, "I know that. Quit spitting in my ear."

Hattie looked past the Whisperer to find Dora June looking back at her. They reached up at the same moment, each tugging an ear. It eased Hattie's concern over grown-ups going at it hammer and tongs.

Gram Julia came that afternoon for a stay. Hattie hoped she could go to school. Instead, she went to the cornfield with Poppa, a wooden peg strapped over her gloved hand. The peg was to tear open the shucks.

Poppa's work-tough hands were faster than Hattie's. She hurried to keep up as the team pulled the corn wagon along. Thunk, thunk, thunk. From sunup until sundown, the shucked corn ears hit the backboard and fell into the wagon. Hattie wore the ends out of her gloves. The wind stung her eyes. Her cheeks peeled and made new freckles over the coming days until her face turned russet, like the apple trees.

Apples, apples! Mama and Gram filled the air with their fragrance, making apple butter over an open fire, then cider of windfalls. They gathered wild grapes and walnuts. They made soap one day and candles another. When Mama was strong enough for the work involved, Poppa took time from corn picking to butcher a hog. Night after night passed, everyone was too tired for a walk to the crying stones.

Then one evening they all went. Hattie traced Louisa's name with a pretty feather and left it at the foot of the stone cross. She left a little pumpkin, too. Then she raced Poppa home and Mama and Gram sat down to quilt. The Jacob's Ladder quilt was eye-catching.

Mama had revised the pattern, altering the squares. Now the steps of the ladder zigzagged instead of running straight like train rails. Freedom's Tracks, zigzagging from hiding place to hiding place. That was Hattie's name for it. She didn't say it out loud, though. Pierce never had given her a straight answer as to whether Grandfather knew that Mama and Poppa helped fugitive slaves.

"Aren't you going to help us?" asked Gram.

Hattie tried. But her fingers were chapped and sore from shucking corn. They kept snagging the fabric.

Gram Julia stayed long enough to see the quilt out of the frame and neatly bound. The following morning Poppa hitched up the team to take her home. Mama clung to Gram as they said good-bye.

"Thanks for coming, Julia," she said finally, and let her go.

Hattie hugged Gram, too. "Tell Pierce to come see how fast I'm getting at picking corn."

"He'll be along with the boys for roundup before you know it. You can show him then," said Gram Julia.

The longhorns left to fatten on the prairie nearby would be cut in with Grandfather's other market-ready cattle up at Funks Grove. Grandfather's annual trail drive was just around the corner. But first, there was the corn harvest to complete.

Autumn rains and falling temperatures made uphill work of it.

Hattie fell asleep at the supper table one night. She awoke awhile later to find Poppa had carried her to bed. The door between her room and the main cabin was open. Poppa was reading by the fire. Mama was mending a ravel in the tulip quilt and wondering aloud over Lizzy.

"I thought we would see her again by now. Do you think she's had trouble?"

"It's too soon to worry."

"I'm not worried," said Mama, and then, in the next breath, "Winter's coming."

"There are other routes," said Poppa.

"I know," said Mama. "All of them longer."

"It's not a thing to be rushed."

"No, it's not." Mama sat down on the bed. She rested a hand over her tummy and closed her eyes.

Hattie closed hers, too, and dreamed of Louisa. When she awoke again, it was daylight and Mama was standing by her bed. She had a freshly pressed dress in hand. "It's time you went back to school."

Dora June's eyes lit up at the sight of Hattie. She threw both hands both in the air, waving. The days passed with no mention of bloodhounds and settled into a familiar routine. Maralee got in the middle of their play more often than not. But Hattie honored Miss Garnet's peacekeeping efforts and made the best of it.

Friday, on the way home from school with Dora June at her side, Hattie found a dried milkweed pod. It was bursting with soft downy fiber. "Louisa's hair was soft like this. Mama said she would have had freckles."

"Louisa is a purty name."

"She *was* pretty." Hattie told Dora June about her being too tiny to breathe. She explained about helping bathe and dress her. "I guess I'm not going to have any sisters or brothers until I get to heaven."

"Me, either," said Dora June. "But that's all right. We got each other. We're sister-friends. For keeps. All right?"

"Sister-friends," agreed Hattie.

Poppa was chopping wood in the yard when Hattie

arrived home. She waved good-bye to Dora June and lingered in the cold sunshine. Poppa grew taller as the ax came up. His muscles gathered beneath his shirt. His wrist veins stood out. In unison came the downward stride and the sound of Poppa exhaling. The flow was smooth, the ringing ax, the flying chips. Hattie stroked milkweed silk with its pinchy seeds, thinking first of Dora June and then of Louisa.

Louisa would never hear Poppa's ax or stroll with Mama or sit on the stoop with a pig in her lap. Yet she had done something Hattie couldn't. Something Mama wouldn't for fear it was selfish. She had kept Poppa home from Kansas Territory. For a while anyway.

Hattie gave up her bed to Miss Garnet the next week. Her room, too. She slept in the trundle bed next to her parents' bed. The bed was too short for her. But it was mid-autumn and cool enough that she liked being close to the fire.

On the last night of Miss Garnet's stay, Hattie awoke to the sound of wheels rolling past the house. She turned over to see Mama leaving the cabin, carrying bedding. Poppa followed, a bucket swinging from each hand.

Runaways! Hattie's pulse ticked in the silence of their going. Could it be Lizzy?

In the next room, covers rustled. Miss Garnet, turning over in her sleep. *Or had she heard the wagon, too?* What if she saw Mama and Poppa helping fugitive slaves?

Hattie crept to the wall partitioning off Miss Garnet's room. Her fingertips explored the hand-hewn logs, looking for the knothole by firelight.

"Mrs. Crosby?"

Hattie leaped away from the wall as if the creek had cracked underfoot. Miss Garnet called again. Afraid she'd get curious and investigate, Hattie whispered, "Did you want something, Miss Garnet?"

"Hattie? Is everything all right?"

"Yes, I'm sleeping is all."

"I thought I heard someone go out."

"That was Poppa. He's checking on the horses," Hattie said, making up an excuse.

"I see," said Miss Garnet finally. "All right, then. Good night, Hattie."

"Good night," said Hattie.

Outside, the sound of wheels and plodding horses faded away. Miss Garnet surely heard them, too. But she didn't call out again. Did she believe Poppa was seeing about horses? Or had she guessed the truth?

Chapter Twenty-Four

Hattie grabbed her shoes from the hearth and slipped outside. The sharp air made clouds of her breath as she circled the barn and found the broken board. She crawled through and into Angel's stall.

A lantern burned in the central corridor of the barn. Mama was serving johnnycakes from the bucket to two girls huddled in the straw with the tulip quilt spread over their laps. Hattie was about to call out to her when she saw a woman over by the door, stripped to the waist, washing herself.

Scars lay upon the woman's back like twisted cords. Hattie's skin went hot and cold and hot again. It was like walking barefoot over a field writhing with snakes. She couldn't step forward. She couldn't step back and erase it from her mind. She shrank to the straw-strewn floor, shivering. By and by, the woman moved from the door and sat down with the two girls. "It's good to be back," she told Mama, and thanked her for the food.

Hattie recognized Lizzy's voice before she did her face. Were these her girls, then? The ones Mama said she would risk so much to rescue? They wore tow-linen dresses and ragged shawls. The smaller of the two had on red shoes. They poked from beneath the quilt.

"It's Hagar's foot gave us trouble," said Lizzy as she ate.

"She got it caught under a cart wheel back on the plantation. We couldn't steal away, not until she had two strong feet. Someone saw me and snitched to Old Master. I made like I'd come back on my own. Told him I was sorry for runnin' before, that I'd as leave be a slave with my girls than free without them."

"Did he believe you?" asked Mama.

"Hard to tell it by the overseer's whip. He like to wore me out."

Mama's breath caught. "Do you need care?" she asked and moved to look.

"It's healing jest fine, missy," said Lizzy.

The girls had finished eating. They put their plates aside and pored over the quilt. The older of the two, named Naomi, traced a tulip. Her lips moved as she whispered words over and over the way Hattie did when she had to memorize a poem for school. Hagar was talking to herself, too, and trailing her finger over irregular stitches. Lizzy oversaw them with an eye just as keen as Miss Garnet at school. She used her fork like a hickory stick, pointing out a crossed stem, a curved petal, and white background thick with stitches, talking low all the while. The girls' eyes and fingers never left the quilt. Their brows furrowed the way Poppa's did when he studied his map of the road leading to Kansas Territory.

Hattie's mouth went suddenly dry. *Could the quilt be more than a memorial for Mama's baby? Could it also be a treasure map, with freedom the treasure? Was that why Mama always took the quilt to the barn when Lizzy came? Is that what she meant by*

Lizzy showing her children how to be free?

As Lizzy's daughters continued to study on the quilt, Lizzy told Mama about their escape. They had left on a Saturday night, for Sunday was the only day an escape had a chance of going unnoticed. But they were missed and tracked to the river and nearly overtaken by patrollers. It was a passing boatman who saved them. On the opposite shore, a family of free blacks hid them in a cave. A string of such hiding places and helping hands had brought them to Mount Hope.

"Old Master warned me he would send shootin' men if ever I ran off again."

"We've sent his slave catchers home empty-handed before," said Mama to Lizzy. "I wish you could stay and rest a while. I'd put some meat on your bones."

"Rest." Lizzy's black eyes got a distant focus. "Used to work the cotton and think there was rest in freedom. Ain't so. Can't be, not when there's children to deliver."

Mama's hand came to that familiar resting place between heart and ribs. Lizzy's gaze followed. Her eyes darkened in realization. She crossed her arms, hugging her own thin frame. "Another child born, another child gathered home."

Her sympathizing sorrow and Mama's bravely held tears loosened the quicksand holding Hattie. She crawled over a manger and into Mama's arms. Mama patted and sniffed and found her voice.

"What're you doing out of bed?"

"Miss Garnet's awake. I think the wagon woke her."

"Thomas?" said Mama, voice climbing.

"I wouldn't borrow trouble just yet," called Poppa from somewhere above them. "Miss Garnet is pretty keen on minding her own business."

"Stand over there by the door, Hattie, and keep watch," said Mama.

Hattie crossed to the door. She tipped her head back and searched the dark cavern of overhead posts and beams for Poppa.

Mama gathered up plates from Lizzy and her girls. "My brothers will be here in the morning to round up cattle for the trail drive north. I'll hang my Jacob's Ladder quilt where you can see it from above. If there's trouble, I'll jerk it down right quick."

A secret signal! thought Hattie. *Like the ear-tug signal she shared with Dora June.*

A rope ladder tumbled down from the outside wall of a grain room within the barn. It was used for storing corn. Poppa lit a candle. One by one, the women climbed the rope ladder and disappeared through a door high in the grain room's slatted wall. Corn ears showing through the slats way up to the rafters. From where Hattie stood, there was nothing to give away the hidden room above.

Poppa climbed down. Lizzy pulled up the ladder. The candle winked out. The lantern, too. Poppa closed up the barn and returned to the house with Hattie and Mama.

If Miss Garnet was awake on the other side of the wall, she didn't let out a peep.

Chapter Twenty-Five

Miss Garnet packed her valise after breakfast on Friday. Her week with them was up. She was going home with Maralee and Rowdy at the end of the school day.

"Wish you didn't have to go," said Hattie, looking on.

"I'll be back again in a few weeks," said Miss Garnet with a smile. She thanked Mama for her hospitality and left for school without Hattie. It was roundup. Hattie was needed at home.

She was throwing table scraps to Aroma when her uncles arrived. Pierce was with them. Poppa saddled up and joined them to collect Grandfather's longhorns from the prairie. Uncle Silas stayed behind to transact business with the neighbors who had a cow or two they wanted taken to market.

"Mr. Jennings is coming up the road with a couple of steers," said Hattie on her way inside with a basket of eggs.

"Maybe he wouldn't mind taking Miss Garnet's valise when he goes," said Mama. "Run see, would you?"

Hattie trekked out and stood by while Uncle Silas wrote Mr. Jennings an IOU bearing Grandfather's signature. Mr. Jennings visited with Uncle Silas a moment, then followed Hattie inside. Mama was putting hot rocks in a milk bucket.

Mr. Jennings indicated the bucket and asked with a grin, "What's the matter, Ellie? Are your cows giving cold milk?"

Mama smiled. "Hello, Tee. How have you been?"

"Can't complain. What're you doing there, anyway?"

"I'm making myself a warming oven. It's going to be a trick to keep everything warm, all the cooking Hattie and I have to do," said Mama. "Did you see my brother Jack?"

"Just missed him," said Mr. Jennings. "Hattie said something about the schoolmarm's trappings."

"I thought maybe you'd take them while you're here and save her the trouble later," said Mama.

"I could. But I'm on my way to the smithy's," said Mr. Jennings. "Why don't I stop on the way back from Atlanta?"

Mama agreed. Mr. Jennings visited a few minutes, then left. Hattie helped Mama pack food into the milk bucket for Lizzy and her girls. Throughout the morning, the hair rose on Hattie's neck each time a neighbor neared their barn.

The trickle of neighbors with livestock continued late into the afternoon. Hattie's friends dashed to her yard as soon as school let out. Dora June tugged her ear in greeting and joined Hattie on the fence. J. B. and Tennessee ambled to the edge of the west field to watch for the cattle.

Rowdy and Maralee came along on Hasty. Miss Garnet was with them. Rowdy didn't want to go home without first catching a glimpse of the herd. So Miss Garnet stepped inside to visit with Mama. Maralee joined Hattie and Dora June on the fence.

"I hear them coming!" Rowdy dashed over the field on his horse.

"Get back here, Rowdy, before they run you over!" Maralee hollered after him.

The air thickened with dust and cattle calls and cracking whips.

Rowdy whistled and waved one arm in the air as the longhorns poured over a small rise. They appeared docile enough, driven along by the mounted men. But Hattie knew they were unpredictable. Rowdy knew it, too. He trotted back to the fence, out of reach of their horns and tramping hooves. J. B. and Tennessee hurried after him. The cattle milled over the field. A few wandered over the barnyard and into the village as there was no fence to hold them.

Poppa sent Pierce to warn the children to stay in the yard and out of the way.

"It's time I was going anyway," said Tennessee.

"What's your hurry?" asked Rowdy as Tennessee hopped off the fence.

"I have to go to the mill."

"It's a little late now," said Maralee. "Mr. Moore's liable to be locked up before you get there."

"That's all right. I'll take a bedroll and be first in line in the morning."

"Or you can sleep at our house," said Rowdy.

"You better watch it coming across his backyard

after dark," warned Dora June. "Pa liked to strangled himself on Mrs. Jennings's clothesline the other night."

"Was that him? I told Mama I heard something," said Maralee.

"He was trying to catch the dogs," said Dora June.

"What was he hunting?" asked Rowdy.

"Dogs. I just told you. What's so funny about that?" asked Dora June when a grin got away from J. B.

"Nothing," he said, and got his mouth straight. "I'm about due for some hunting myself. How about it, Tenny?" J. B. called after Tennessee. "I'll do chores, then I'll meet you at the mill."

"Me, too," cried Rowdy.

"Mama isn't going to let you in the woods with those two toting guns," said Maralee.

"Who said anything about guns?" said J. B.

"How else are you going to hunt?" asked Maralee.

"Come see," said J. B. "And bring a sack."

Maralee tossed her red hair, all set to get to the bottom of the grins the boys were trading when Miss Garnet came out of the house, ready to go. Mr. Jennings rode up just then with his sharpened plowshares. He took Miss Garnet's bag and Rowdy, too. Miss Garnet mounted up on Hasty.

"Come on, Dora June. There's room," said Maralee.

Hattie's friends went their separate ways.

Pierce swung off his horse and knocked the dust from his hat and long black drover's coat. His belly growled so loud, Hattie laughed.

"I can't help it, I'm starving," he said.

"You better be. We cooked all day."

"*You* cooked?" Pierce made a face and set in teasing on the way to the wash stump.

Hattie was giving him a good splashing when two men rode out of the south on silver-saddled horses. Their pale thigh-length coats and wide-brimmed hats were not those of farmers or neighbors or drovers. But they *were* familiar. The hard cake of lye soap pinched her gripping fingers. "Pierce?"

"I see them." Pierce's tongue flicked to the corner of his mouth.

"Is it . . ."

"The slave hunters," he finished for her. "Hunnicutt and Dungey."

Poppa rode through a sea of cattle to meet the men. Mr. Dungey shifted his rifle across his knees and leaned forward to pat his horse's neck. Mr. Hunnicutt doffed his hat and reached into an inside coat pocket.

"A handbill," said Pierce.

Shootin' men. Lizzy's words banged in Hattie's ears. She bounded around the house, snatched Mama's Freedom Tracks quilt from the line and circled back again.

Her uncles were strung out over field and farm like spokes on a wheel. They turned as one and began working their horses toward Poppa. Bits rattled. Saddle leather creaked. Hooves sucked the dust as Hunnicutt's cold gaze swung from the bill, crumpled on the ground, to Hattie's gathering uncles. His rifle butt skinned the gilded saddle horn as he drew himself taller in the saddle.

But Mr. Dungey cautioned him with a motion of his gloved hand. He pulled ahead on his horse so that he was between Hunnicutt and Poppa. "I apologize on behalf of Mr. Hunnicutt and myself for interrupting your work, gentlemen. You all go on about your business. We'll take *our* business to Constable Carlson."

Abruptly, the men turned their horses and left by the north road. Hattie's uncles converged on Poppa. He spoke to them briefly, then rode to the gate, swung out of the saddle, and tossed Pierce the reins.

Chapter Twenty-Six

Hattie barged through the door ahead of Poppa. "The slave hunters are back!"

Mama's scar leaped white upon her cheek. Her gaze flew from the signal quilt in Hattie's arms to Poppa. "What do they want?"

"A look in the barn," said Poppa. "I told them we were moving cattle, I couldn't show them around. They went for the constable."

"They'll be back with the dogs."

"Yes. But we've bought a little time," said Poppa. "Find them some traveling clothes. Trousers and shirts for the girls."

Mama cleared the top of the blanket chest of overflow dishes she had been preparing all day. She opened the lid and plowed through the donated garments within.

"Cole and Pete will move the girls cross-country with part of the herd," said Poppa. "Silas and Jack and I are going to drive the rest of the cattle up the north road and meet the constable, coming. If we can stall him, it'll be dark before he reaches the farm. Otherwise, he's sure to see the second cattle trail and wonder why we split the herd."

Mama turned with a pile of clothes in arm. "What about Lizzy?"

"You'll have to see her on her way while Pierce covers their tracks and erases all trace of them from the barn."

Mama peeled off her apron and reached for her cape.

"Keep her out of sight once you get to the station. Don't let her board until the train is ready to pull out," warned Poppa. He turned to Hattie. "Help your mother, then come back and wait for me by the gate. You'll have to come with me."

At Mama's instruction, Hattie packed roasted quail, apples, and corn dodgers into a bucket. She hurried out to the barn where Lizzy and her girls were dressed for flight. Lizzy wore Hattie's sunbonnet, Hattie's cape, and beneath it, a calico dress. Naomi and Hagar wore drover's coats and hats over jeans and loose-fitting hunting shirts. They ate the meat standing up and poked the apples and corn dodgers into their pockets.

"You look like drovers. Except for those red shoes." Hattie's gaze shifted from Hagar's red shoes to Mama.

"They'll have to do. We're out of time, and it's too cold for her to go barefooted," said Mama.

Hattie wiggled her toes in her own black shoes. They looked close in size. "You want to trade?"

Hagar slipped off the red shoes. Quickly, the trade was made.

"That's better," said Mama. "Thank you, Hattie. Take their clothes to the cabin and burn them. Make sure there's no food left on the fire, bank it, and close up the cabin."

The tulip quilt was among the discarded clothes. Hattie offered it to the girls, thinking they might need it for the journey. But Lizzy wouldn't let them take it. "They's more to come," she said.

Though Lizzy didn't say it in words, Hattie knew then that without a doubt the quilt was a picture to freedom for those who knew Lizzy's stitching language and could carry what they had "read" in their minds.

Hattie saw, as she raced back to the house, something new on the quilt. Lizzy had embroidered Naomi and Hagar's names into the border. She padded her hand with a corner of it and pulled the iron pots and kettles away from the fire before throwing the slave clothes in.

Poppa called to her from the gate. "Are you ready, Hattie?"

"Mama said knock the fire down."

"I can't wait. You and Pierce will have to catch up," he said, and then he was gone.

Hattie banked the fire. She threw the tulip quilt around her shoulders, tied opposite corners across her chest, and poked her apron pocket full of corn dodgers. Mama and Lizzy were galloping south on Angel as Hattie stepped out of the cabin. Lizzy had her face pressed against Mama's back so it was hidden.

Uncle Cole rode to the barn and stretched a hand to Hagar. Naomi, the older of the two, swung up on Pierce's horse and followed. They rode east through Mount Hope, getting the cattle moving. Uncle Pete brought up the rear. One of the girls was wearing his coat and hat. He made do with a blanket, worn poncho-style.

"H-e-e y-a-a-h!" Uncle Pete hurried the cattle along with a shout and snap of his stockman's whip.

Poppa, Uncle Silas, and Uncle Jack started a second group of cattle up the road the slave hunters had taken. As the dust settled, Hattie circled the cabin. Pierce hailed her from the barn. Like Uncle Pete, he had given up his coat and hat.

"Help me scatter the straw and run the hogs into the barn," he called to her.

Hattie raced to help. Pierce turned one of Poppa's work horses out of the barn for them to ride while she scattered straw.

"You're going to freeze. I'll run and get another quilt," she offered, and cast the hay fork aside.

Pierce was closing Aroma into the barn with the rest of the hogs when Hattie returned with the quilt. He wrapped it around his shoulders and mounted up. They started north out of Mount Hope. They hadn't gone far when Hattie heard a squeal and looked back to see Aroma following.

"Oh, no! Stop, Pierce."

"How'd *he* get out?"

"There's a broken board along the back wall. He must have found it."

"I suppose we have to take him back," grumbled Pierce.

"We can't leave him wandering. He'll get lost," said Hattie. The gulf between them and the cattle was a wide one. Feeling pulled both ways, she added, "Poppa's going to wonder what's happened to us if we turn back, though."

"You keep going, then. I'll take him back," said Pierce.

Hattie climbed down and divided the corn dodgers. Pierce broke one into pieces, and used it to coax Aroma back the way they had come. Hattie plodded along wearing blisters on her heels from the ill-fitting shoes. By and by, Pierce caught up with her again. Hattie mounted up behind him and asked about Aroma.

"I rolled a heavy log in front of the board. He won't get loose again," said Pierce. "Hang on, I'll catch us up."

They were trailing the herd when Mr. Dungey and Mr. Hunnicutt crested the hill. Poppa veered to the west side of the herd. The slave hunters rode to meet him. Uncle Silas swung in the same direction. Pierce started that way, too, then pulled up short.

"Bloodhounds," he said, and pointed.

The dogs came weaving over the hill from Johnson's Grove to the north, sweeping the ground with their noses. Mr. Carlson was at their heels. Poppa rode to meet him. The conversation was brief. The constable backed away with the dogs and cut wide to the west, and then south again toward Mount Hope.

"What's he doing?" asked Hattie.

"Getting those dogs past without spooking the cattle," said Pierce. "If he stampedes them, he will answer to Father."

Poppa rode back to meet Pierce and Hattie. His eyes

glinted in his dusty face. "We have to take the cattle back to the farm. Constable Carlson is making us help look for the fugitive slaves these men are seeking," he said as the slave hunters caught up.

"Uncle Jack and Uncle Silas, too?" asked Pierce.

"He says he'll charge us if we refuse," said Poppa, words clipped. "You'll have to look after the cattle once we get them back to the farm, Pierce. Hattie, walk to Tee Jennings's place and see if he'll come help Pierce. It'll be dark soon, so don't dawdle," he warned.

Hattie slid off the horse. She made a wide sweep, staying well away from the cattle as Uncle Jack, Uncle Silas, Poppa, and Pierce turned them back toward Mount Hope. The dust settled behind them. The bellowing faded to a distant lonely coo and she was alone.

Chapter Twenty-Seven

The sky shifted from rose to lavender and then to slate as Hattie followed the trail north toward Johnson's Grove. As darkness fell, she was less sure of the familiar path. Her heel hurt and a hooting owl made her jump. But Poppa was counting on her. Pierce, too.

The moon was up by the time she reached Johnson's Grove. Tee Jennings and his family lived in the woods not far from Moore's Mill. Fallen leaves rustled underfoot. Chafing branches creaked overhead. Migrating geese gabbled from some far-off field.

Hattie paused to pad her sore heel with a folded leaf. Yips and whines sounded in the distance and rose to short staccato barks. *Bloodhounds?* No one but Mr. Carlson had bloodhounds and he was taking them to search the farm. Their cries would not carry all the way from Mount Hope to Johnson's Grove.

Hattie tugged at the shoe, trying to stretch it. As she worked her foot in, every nerve in her body went still. *The shoes*. Had she laid a trail for the dogs with her traded shoes? Were the bloodhounds following her?

The dogs' howls went deep, like fiddles hitting all bass notes. A speck of yellow light glimmered through the trees. They *were* coming. They were coming for her.

Hattie ran away from the light, over a log and

through underbrush. A thorn gashed her shoe. She pulled it from her throbbing foot and limped on as the baying swelled. Branches tore at her quilt. Undergrowth tripped her.

She stumbled into a leaning tree. It was uprooted, but its branches were tangled in those of a neighboring tree. The trunk, steeply pitched, was cold and musky with decay.

Hattie's fingernails sank into rotting wood as she clawed her way upward. She was well off the ground when the lantern glimmered below. It wasn't slave hunters. It was Rowdy.

"Rowdy," she cried. "Up here!"

"Freckles?" Rowdy dropped his head back. "What're you doing?"

"I was coming to see your poppa. I hear dogs. Hear them?"

"That's just Mr. Carlson working his bloodhounds." Rowdy held up the lantern. His face split into a big grin. "Guess what? There aren't any snipe. J. B. and Tenny were having a joke on me. But they got joked, too. Miss Garnet came to the mill to fetch me home for supper. She slipped up on the boys beating the bushes. It gave them such a fright, they 'bout jumped out of their britches."

"Hattie?" Miss Garnet stepped into the smudge of light and tipped her face. "What are you doing here?"

"Mr. Carlson's making Poppa and my uncles look for runaways. Pierce is all alone with the cattle. Poppa wants Mr. Jennings to go to Mount Hope and help him keep the herd together until they get back."

"If the constable *is* on the trail of fugitive slaves, this is no place for children," said Miss Garnet, alarm in her voice. "Come down from there, Hattie, and we'll go give Mr. Jennings your father's message."

The dogs' baying, ever closer, shivered through Hattie like beating wings wrapped around piercing cries. She inched higher, even as Miss Garnet urged her to hurry.

Rowdy gave Miss Garnet the lantern and scrambled up the barkless log. "Come on, Freckles. I'll help you down." He caught her foot and yanked so hard, her shoe came off in his hand.

"Don't pull on her, Rowdy. You'll both fall!"

The rest of Miss Garnet's warning was lost to the thundering dogs and thrashing underbrush and clashing voices. The wood beneath Hattie groaned and creaked as the overhead branches snapped and slid out of their forked cradle. The rotting tree trunk shuddered, then twisted. Hattie fell with a shower of limbs and broken timber.

Time seemed to slow and stretch out forever. It was as if she were a leaf, floating in a maddening crawl to the ground. Below her, Miss Garnet lifted her arms. The lantern she held aloft lit her horror as bloodhounds lunged out of darkness.

Chests heaving.

Frothing jaws sharp with teeth.

Men at their heels.

Hattie hit the trembling earth and rolled.

Away from the dogs, frenzied by flames.

Poppa battled through limbs and rotted wood. He scooped her from the littered ground.

Flames licked at Miss Garnet's clothes. Her screams tore the air.

Men sprang to help. But her legs were pinned by limbs.

Rowdy was pinned, too. Beneath the rotted trunk. He wasn't talking. He wasn't moving. His still hand held Hattie's red shoe.

Chapter Twenty-Eight

Uncle Jack carried Rowdy home on horseback.

Hattie rode the short distance with Poppa.

Uncle Silas and the others followed on foot. They used Hattie's quilt as a litter to carry Miss Garnet.

Hattie stayed at the Jenningses' home while Poppa went to get Doctor Proctor for Miss Garnet. There was nothing to be done for Rowdy. The tree had crushed him.

Hattie huddled near the fire with nothing to hold on to but the love of Poppa's heart-failing look as he pulled her out of broken branches.

Shock and grief rocked the room around her as Mrs. Jennings gathered Rowdy in her arms. Maralee sank to the floor beside her mother and buried her face in her skirts. Each wail of anguish cut Hattie like an ax. She couldn't stop shaking. She couldn't escape. There was no one to help her past the dogs in the yard.

Uncle Silas poured something down Miss Garnet to numb her pain as she waited for the doctor to arrive. Uncle Jack tried to comfort his old friend, Mr. Jennings.

"He was just here," said Mr. Jennings as if he could not make sense of Rowdy, so still in his mother's arms. He shook Uncle Jack's arm off his shoulder. "How did this happen? How could it happen?"

The constable stammered tearful apologies.

Mr. Dungey spoke words of regret, too. Like Mr. Carlson, he couldn't explain why the dogs had struck a false trail that had led to such tragic consequences. Mr. Hunnicutt, when questioned, said that he had been at the edge of the woods, holding the horses as the others followed the dogs on foot.

"You should have let us know you were searching," said Mr. Jennings. "We'd have got our boy out of harm's way."

"Begging your pardon, sir. You see how easily they slip through our fingers," said Mr. Dungey. "There is no time for alerting the neighborhood."

"We're law-abiding folk, we don't harbor runaways. Why would they come here? Why would they do this to us?" sobbed Mrs. Jennings.

Hattie shivered and closed her eyes. Scars were etched on her eyelids. Lizzy's scars. Lizzy's face. Lizzy's naked back.

Hattie didn't want to go to the burial. Mama insisted.

"Poppa and I will be right there with you. You'll feel better for going," she said.

Hattie didn't see how that could be. But she went. Afterward, she stood with Maralee while Mama hugged Maralee's mother in wordless consolation.

Maralee knotted a wet handkerchief between her fingers and wiped her eyes with her hand. "I was supposed to go get him, but Miss Garnet said she'd go."

"It wasn't your fault." Hattie said the same words

Mama had been saying to her in the three days since the accident.

"I wish I had gone. Maybe it would have been different if I had been there," said Maralee.

Mama, in trying to soothe Hattie, had said that it was no good visiting the Maybes. She had said that it was decayed hearts that had brought those men into the woods with dogs. She reasoned that had it been Lizzy's child who had died, they would have ridden away with their heads up, patting the necks of their proud horses instead of leaving in the night as they had done. But none of that would help Maralee.

Hattie gave Maralee her spare handkerchief. She had nothing else to give.

In the coming days, it appeared that Mr. Carlson was visiting the Maybes, too. Or perhaps the growl of the community, up in arms over the tragedy, was too much for him. He packed up a week after the funeral and went back to Kentucky, taking Dora June and Auntie Carlson with him. There was no chance for good-byes or even an ear tug.

Miss Garnet's condition stabilized. They moved her by wagon to the doctor's home for what turned out to be a lengthy recovery. Uncle Silas visited her frequently. He didn't mention changes in her appearance. But others did. It was rumored she was disfigured and could not walk and would never teach again.

There was a qualified teacher in McLean, the village born beside the railroad tracks three miles to the east.

But they had no building. So in February, when the pumpkin Hattie had left on Louisa's grave was sunken and cased in ice, the men of the neighborhood moved the old Congregational church, which had served Mount Hope both as sanctuary and school. Hattie watched twenty-four yoke of oxen pull it across the snowy prairie toward McLean. It was like watching a lamp sputter and burn out, for with it went all that remained of Mount Hope.

What was there to hold Poppa now? His long ago New England-on-the-prairie dream was dead. He was speaking of Kansas again.

Chapter Twenty-Nine

Spring 1857

"Hattie? Poppa says five minutes," called Mama from the front yard.

Hattie tossed Aroma a good-bye dandelion. "Remember, now. If Uncle Silas tries to take you to market, you head out for Kansas Territory. That's west past Missouri."

Aroma wasn't listening. He was an uncle now, and not a very good one. He knocked little pigs away from the trough with a churlish sweep of his head. He was, by any name, just a selfish pig.

"Good-bye, chickens," said Hattie. "Good-bye, fence. Good-bye, garden."

Mama was by the wagon, hugging her brothers one by one. She saved Grandfather and Gram Julia for last. But she didn't cry and she didn't cling. Hattie wasn't going to disgrace herself with tears, either.

"I want you to promise me you will at least think about coming back once Kansas enters the Union," said Gram Julia to Poppa.

"We'll see," said Poppa.

Gram Julia kissed him, then Hattie, and whispered, "It's hard on your mama, leaving everything behind.

How about you? Are you going to be all right?"

"I'll be fine," said Hattie. "I love you, Gram."

"I love you, too."

Uncle Silas kissed Hattie's hand when she finally got to him. It made her feel so grown-up, she forgot to make him agree never to turn Aroma into ham, bacon, or sausage.

Miss Garnet was beside him. She was walking again with the help of a cane. But the old swing-swang was missing and her burns had left scars. They trailed from the ridge of her left cheek, under her chin to disappear in the white frills at her throat. Her eyes brightened with tears as Hattie told her good-bye.

"Use your head and not your fingers for your times tables. I want your new friends in Kansas to know you have received a good education."

"I will," promised Hattie. "I'll be considerate, too, like you said. And I'll only talk about nice things that people can agree on."

Miss Garnet's smile faltered. "Sometimes, Hattie, there are not so nice things that need to be talked about, too. Things upon which people won't agree. You say what is true and don't let anyone stir you from it."

Hattie could see she was wishing for a chance to do some things over, too. She hugged her and whispered, "Mama says don't visit the Maybes."

"She told me, too. She's right, you know. They make poor hosts. They kick you about and take and never give," said Miss Garnet.

"Oh! I almost forgot. I made you something." Hattie

raced inside for the bustle and out again. She had wrapped it in a tow-linen dishcloth. "You can open it later."

"Are you sure you don't want me to open it now?"

"You better wait." Hattie rose on tiptoe and dropped her voice to a whisper. "It's an unmentionable. For your swing-swang."

Red swept up Miss Garnet's scarred throat all the way to her cheeks. "I see," she said. "Perhaps it would be best to wait."

"I made it myself. All but the feathers. Those came from Maralee. It's to remember us by. Dora June, too," added Hattie.

"That's very sweet," said Miss Garnet. She hugged Hattie and kissed her cheek. "I'm going to miss you, Hattie. I have so been looking forward to being your aunt."

"Me, too," said Hattie. "I had a bad dream once. I dreamed you married old Long Whiskers."

"Hattie, what have I told you about that?" scolded Mama.

Uncle Silas chuckled. "Now that *would* have been a tragedy," he said, and slipped an arm around Miss Garnet

Miss Garnet smiled up at him, and in that moment, was beautiful again. They planned to marry next month and farm Poppa's farm and live in Hattie's house until they could build one of their own.

"Be sure and keep Lizzy's quilt up in the window, Silas," Mama was saying. "I want her to know it's still a safe house, even though we're not here."

And those she brought would need to study the quilt's secrets, thought Hattie. Mama passed the stained and mended tulip quilt to Uncle Silas.

"I hope she brings us some more drovers when she comes," said Uncle Cole with a grin. "Those last two were pretty fair cowboys by the time we got to the stock-yards."

Grandfather and the boys had smuggled Lizzy's girls north on the trail drive and sent them the rest of the way north by steamboat. Poppa had received word from friends in the Canadian town where the girls were living that they were looking forward to the day when Lizzy could join them. But, so far, there had been no word of Lizzy. Mama said there would always be children for Lizzy to deliver. She said Lizzy couldn't be truly free when others were not. What did that mean, "truly free"?

Uncle Pete swung Hattie up over the wheel toward Mama before she had time to think it through. "So long, Snipe. Don't let the prairie dogs get you."

Hattie turned on the seat, looking down at Pierce. "Are prairie dogs real? Or is that a greenhorn joke?"

"What are you asking me for? I've never been to Kansas. Yet," added Pierce.

"Is it, Uncle Cole? Uncle Pete! Tell me!"

The boys laughed and started making up stories, both of them talking at the same time. Poppa shook the lines. Their covered wagon rolled ahead. Mama was calm and resolute. She didn't look back at the crying stones or the boys or Gram and Grandfather or Hattie's soon-to-be Aunt Harmony. Her eyes were dry and her hand was on Poppa's knee as they set off for "bleeding" Kansas.

Hattie kept her head up and her eyes dry, too. She had gone to the cemetery with Mama last evening. New grass and wildflowers grew amidst last year's decomposing growth. On Louisa's grave, twin pumpkin leaves had pushed through the ground like praying hands. Come fall, there would be pumpkins. She wouldn't be here to see them, but it pleased Hattie to think of life coming from that one dead pumpkin. Perhaps there would be a whole patch of pumpkins when she returned, grown and free to do as she pleased. And she *would* return. Mount Hope had not seen the last of Hattie Crosby.

Epilogue

Lacey traced broken threads and frayed seams in the old quilt in Gram's lap. Intrigued, she asked, "So is it a memory quilt? Or is it a map?"

"It's both and more, depending upon who is reading it," said Gram.

"Can you?" asked Lacey.

"I can read the love and the courage."

"But not the map?"

"No," admitted Gram. "But I've often wondered if the squares were a grid, representing a certain number of miles. As for the directions, they could be coded in the stitches and knots. And did you notice how some flowers touch the border and others don't?"

"Why? Is it important?"

"It would be if it indicated a turn or a safe house or danger ahead."

Lacey studied the quilt until her eyes blurred, but she could only guess at the map hidden there. "It's a good thing I didn't live back then. I wouldn't know where to begin to make a map of cloth."

"Because you don't need to. But if your life depended upon it, I think you'd get pretty creative." Gram snipped a thread and rose to put the mended quilt away.

"Did Hattie come back?" asked Lacey, trailing after her.

"To Illinois? Yes, though not until she was a young woman. By then, the cabin was gone, and the little cemetery was all that remained of Mount Hope."

"It was sad about Rowdy and baby Louisa," murmured Lacey.

"Didn't I warn you there was heartache stitched in?"

"What about Lizzy? Did she make it to Canada?"

"No. Gram Hattie's family received word of her after the war. Lizzy settled with a daughter in a little town in Oklahoma. She remained there for the rest of her life."

"Did Miss Garnet ever get her swing-swang back?"

Gram chuckled. "I don't know about that. But she raised seven children and a grandson, too."

"How am I related to her, again?"

"You aren't, by blood. She was Pierce's step-mom," reminded Gram. "Pierce is your great-great-great-grandfather on Max's side."

Great-Grandfather Max Tandy was Gram's late husband. Lacey knew his face from photographs, but didn't remember him.

"It's quite a lot to hold in your head. But the quilt you're making will help. Let's cut out a sunbonnet girl for Hattie."

"She liked yellow, right?" said Lacey. "And I'll use bottle green for Harmony. What is bottle green, anyway?"

"I believe it is somewhere between olive, jade, and jealous."

"Gram!"

Gram chuckled. "I'm getting ahead of myself. I was about to tell you what the flaw was."

"That's easy. Slavery," said Hattie.

"Go a little deeper," urged Gram.

Lacey made her voice deep. "Slavery."

Gram peered over her glasses.

"I heard that from Sheri," said Lacey, grinning.

"See there? Sisters can be fun."

"Sometimes they're okay. So what was the flaw?"

"Failure to treat others the way you yourself would want to be treated. It goes clear back to the Constitution," said Gram. "The framers representing Northern states wanted Congress to abolish the slave trade. Southern delegates disagreed. So they compromised. They compromised truth and justice. The result was a flawed foundation trying to bear the weight of a new and diverse nation. That's a little like piecing a quilt without first prewashing your fabrics. First time you wash it, the dyes in the cloth bleed all over one another. And what do you have to show for your time and trouble?"

"A mess," said Lacey. Quickly she added, "I hope my quilt doesn't bleed."

"It won't," Gram reassured her. "I wash all my fabrics until the water runs clear."

Relieved, Lacey's thoughts turned from cloth, compromises, and the Constitution to Judith's breakfast announcement. "Did Hattie ever get another sister?"

"No, honey, she didn't. Pioneer life was pretty

difficult," said Gram. "But of course she did have babies of her own when she was grown and married to Grampa Matthew. My mother, Anna, was the youngest in the family. Gram Hattie lived with us the last few years of her life. That's how we came to be so close."

Lacey put Gram's thimble on her finger and gave it a twist. Round and round and round until finally the words came out: "Judith's going to have a baby. Did you know?"

Gram smiled. "Yes. Your father told me. Are you excited?"

Lacey shrugged. "We're crowded already. I don't know where we'll find room for a baby."

"Just as long as there's room in your heart," said Gram. She patted Lacey's hand. "It will mean change, of course. But whatever you have to give up in space and time and attention won't seem like much for what you get in return."

"What?" asked Lacey.

Gram beamed. "A brand new Tandy to love."

"But what if it doesn't . . . what if I don't . . . never mind," said Lacey, ashamed to admit even to Gram her fear this new baby might crowd her out of her father's heart.

"Love's a funny thing," said Gram, closing the lid on the quilt trunk. "Sometimes, it just grips you by the heart and you love as easy as you breathe. But sometimes, it starts in your head. You make up your mind to love, and the feeling follows."

"How?" asked Lacey.

"I can't explain. It's a work of faith, I guess. But it *does* work, I promise," added Gram.

Lacey thought of all the fine stories Gram told her of ancestors gone from this world. Her words gave them life. Even baby Louisa. She had not seen or held her or even touched her crying stone. Yet she was real to Lacey. More real than this baby who was coming.

"Another thing about love," said Gram Jennie as she led the way to the kitchen. There's always enough to go around."

"Like cake?" asked Lacey.

Gram cocked her head inquiringly.

"The more there are to eat it, the smaller Judith cuts the pieces."

Gram Jennie smiled and put an arm around Lacey. "No, honey. Love isn't like cake. Love multiplies upon itself. It just grows and grows. Trust me, you'll see."

✱ AMERICAN QUILTS SERIES ✱

Activity Pages by Stasia Kehoe

BOOK 2: HATTIE's STORY

Make a Memory: Memento Box

Lizzie's quilt bears the names of her freed children and the black lines of "Jacob's Ladder"—a symbol of the road to freedom. You, too, can create a very personal memento. You will need:

A small cardboard box

Tracing paper

A pencil

Felt

Colorful fabric scraps

Scissors

Craft glue

A fabric-friendly paint pen

Ribbons, buttons, dried flowers, or other craft materials

Remove the lid from the box. Use the pencil to trace the shape of the lid, bottom, and sides of the box onto tracing paper. Cut out the shapes and then retrace them onto the felt. (Hint: Use a pin to secure the traced pattern onto the felt.) Carefully glue the felt inside the box to make a pretty lining. Line only the top of the lid, as lining the sides will make the box hard to close. Choose your favorite colored scraps of fabric to decorate the outside of the box. Cut the fabric and/or more felt into meaningful shapes, such as initials or pet silhouettes. When the glue is dry, use the pen to write important names or other special messages. Glue on ribbons, buttons, or other decorations. Fill your personalized memento box with very special treasures.

Quilting Corner: A Modern-Day Quilting Bee

Hattie's family gets together when it is time to finish a quilt. They share stories, recipes, laughter, and the work of putting quilt squares together to make a lasting blanket. Think of a community service you and your friends or family could perform together, such as picking up litter from the park, baking cookies to take to a senior citizen center, or putting on a play for local preschoolers. When your activity is finished, ask each person to commemorate his or her effort by decorating a "quilt square" of colored paper (about 12" X 12") with drawings, photographs, or a short written paragraph. Using a hand-held punch, make holes about 2" apart around the edges of each square. Lay the squares out on a flat surface, then "sew" them together by lacing colored yarn through the holes. Hang your finished quilt for all to enjoy.

School Stories: Boarding Around

In *Hattie's Story*, Miss Garnet boards around, living with the families of each of her students in turn. This was a common arrangement for frontier teachers. Imagine that you are Miss Garnet, far from your own home, living with a different family every few weeks. As Miss Garnet, you keep a journal. Write two journal entries, one about boarding with Hattie Crosby's family and one about staying with Dora June Carlson. Describe each home and family and how you feel about staying with them. What secrets might you accidentally discover? What if the people with whom you are staying believe differently than you about slavery, child rearing, manners, or other matters?

Family Tree Time: Make a Face Familiar

Gram and her quilts help to make the people from Lacey's past come to life. You, too, can turn an old family name into a living, breathing person. Ask an older relative to tell you a childhood story about him or herself, or about a favorite grandparent you never had a chance to meet. Find a photograph of this person or draw a picture based on the description you hear. Write his or her story down. Then go to your school library or media center to add detail to the story. Find out about the town in which his or her story took place, key historical events happening at the time, even what the weather was like that year. Your past will come alive just like it does for Lacey Tandy.

Presenting the Past: The Civil War

The 1850s and '60s were a turbulent time in American history. Some people thought that white people had a right to own slaves, while others believed that people of all races and colors were entitled to their freedom. The slave issue pitted neighbor against neighbor, brother against brother, and friend against friend. It threatened to destroy the United States of America. Go to your local library or online to learn more about America's Civil War, the Underground Railroad, and about Abraham Lincoln, who makes an appearance in *Hattie's Story* and who, in the real history of the United States, played a vital role in ending slavery.

American Quilt Questions: Friends and Family

In *Hattie's Story*, conflict between their families' feelings about slavery sours Hattie and Dora June's friendship.

Why does Dora June feel she must be mean to Hattie?

How do you think being an only child in 1856 was similar to being an only child today? How might it have been different?

Do you think being an only child makes the trouble with Dora June especially hard for Hattie? Explain.

Hattie tells her teacher: "I have brothers, they just didn't stay to play." How does this sentence help readers understand Hattie's personality?

Hattie is happy when she and Dora June agree to be "sister-friends." Do you have a friend so special you think of her as a sister? Describe this friendship.

Do you think you could be friends with someone whose family held beliefs very different from your own? Why or why not?

BOOK 3: DANIEL's STORY

Daniel Tandy was dark-eyed, scant, and scrawny. He was a comma in a compound sentence of land-rich Tandys. His father was a question mark off taming the wild west. His mother was underground. And his grandparents were periods.

"Grampa?" said Daniel one morning as he poured over his sketchbook. "I was thinking I'd go visit Dad when it gets to be summer."

"South Dakota?" Grampa Silas unfolded himself from his chair by the stove. "I'm too old, and you're too young to cross the country alone."

Period. Fixed and firm as a mended fence. If he wouldn't reach into his deep pockets, asking Gram Harmony was a waste of breath.

Commas bend. Sometimes they yield. But they have heels, by hook. Without a word, Daniel dug his in. He would go to South Dakota if he had to sketch his way there.

Robinlike, Daniel kept his ear to the ground. Late in January, the worm wiggled. The worm came by way of Jack, who was Daniel's best friend and the grandson of Gramp Silas's stepbrother, Jack Tandy.

"Earl's going to make syrup next month. You want to help?" Jack asked.

That easy, the means of earning a ticket west were within Daniel's grasp.

Days later, Daniel tramped through the woods with Jack. Thawing earth and dead leaves bled through the thin, wet snow underfoot. He dropped to one knee, pressed the drill bit into bark and rotated the brace. Maple shavings scattered on the breeze.

Jack charged the hole with a wooden sap spile and hammer. Daniel rubbed a watery eye and walked on. He didn't know maples by bark. But Jack's brother, Earl, had left buckets beneath the trees to be tapped.

"Hey! You're getting ahead of yourself," hollered Jack.

Daniel glanced back and saw he had missed a bucket. He was chilled, his knees wet and muddy clear through his long-handles. "You drill it," he said, and offered Jack the brace and bit.

"You," said Jack. "You're closer to the ground."

Jack was a year older than Daniel, a head taller, and stoutly built.

He squatted like a frog about to jump while Daniel drilled the hole. Jack cleaned out the shavings with a twig and took another spile from the lard pail.

The spiles were as big around as a man's finger. There were long, lightweight and channeled to carry maple sap from the tree to the bucket on the ground. Grampa Silas had helped Earl whittle them from elderberry and sumac. Earl was fresh out of school. Tandylike, he was set on making a living off the land, even if the land was in trees.

"How much is Earl paying us?" asked Daniel.

"Not much. He's cheap." Jack urged the spile into the hole with the hammer, then set the bucket beneath it.

A train rattled by on the nearby Chicago and Alton tracks and slowed for Funks Grove crossing.

"Must be the nooner," said Jack. "My belly's growling."

Daniel wiped his dripping nose. "Want to walk to the store and warm up?"

"I don't have any money."

"We can put some cheese on Grampa's account. He won't care," said Daniel.

Walker's Store was a rough-sawed wood and tin-roofed affair with a wide front window and living quarters in back for young Mr. Walker and his wife. It stood in a clearing near the rural crossing where the tracks ran through sprawling timber.

A handful of men climbed off the train. They pulled coats on over their red bandanas, cinder-pocked shirts, and coveralls. Leaving the tinder taking on water, they ambled toward Walker's. Daniel crossed in front of the idling engine. It hissed and popped and sent a thin ribbon of steam floating into the trees.

Jack dropped his red head back, squinting at the engine. "You ever been up there?"

"No," said Daniel. "Have you?"

"Nope. How about it?"

"You mean, now?"

"Sure, now," said Jack.

"What if they catch us?"

"They won't."

Daniel frowned up at the engine. He shifted from one cold foot to the other.

Jack twisted his mouth to one side and sniffed. "What's that again about your trader, trapper, track-laying, Indian scouting, gold-prospecting daddy?"

"I never said he laid track. I said he hunted buffalo to feed the men who built the railroad across. . . ."

"The plains. I know." Jack bumped Daniel with his shoulder. "So did Fierce Pierce get all the guts in the family?"

Walker's door slammed shut behind the train crew. Daniel eyed the monster engine and gave in with a shrug.

Jack's wind-burned freckles bunched into a grin. He set aside his hammer and pail of spiles and reached for the bottom rung of the steps that scaled the engine. Daniel dropped his tools and scrambled up after him. It was warm inside the engine cab.

"What're you buying with your syrup money?" asked Daniel, thawing his hands at the firebox door.

"Bicycle, maybe." Jack gripped a brass knob. He thunked a gauge. "How about you?"

"I'm going to buy a train ticket to South Dakota."

"To see your dad?"

Daniel nodded.

"Uncle Silas know?"

"No. Don't tell anybody, okay?"

" 'Course not. Tandys never tell on Tandys," said Jack.

It was true. Of Jack, anyway. For all his cajoling and ca-jamming and half-cocked Tandy temper, he was a clam when it came to secrets.

Jack spit on the sooty window and rubbed a patch clean with his coat sleeve. "Look there, a bird's-eye view. Almost see clear to Indian country."

The farm where Daniel lived with his grandparents was a half mile due east. He couldn't see it for the woodlands in between.

Jack nudged him. "Look here, coming. Chaldea."

A woman with flaming hair and flapping black skirts pedaled across Timber Creek bridge on a bicycle. Her name wasn't really Chaldea. Miss Maralee Jennings, that was her name. She lived in the woods and gathered bark and roots and such. What she couldn't find in the wild, she grew and dried for teas and poultices and potions. "Remedies," she called them.

"Earl says she reads the future in the stars," said Jack. "He says when she talks to the dead, they talk back."

"How?"

"Spirit to spirit."

Daniel prodded with the tip of his tongue the space between his front teeth, watching Chaldea's bicycle wobble over thawing ruts. She stopped at the crossing, looked at the train, then south to open track, and pedaled ahead.

The steam whistle shrieked. Daniel jumped.

Chaldea, too. She veered hard to the right. The front wheel of her bicycle jammed between rail and rocks. She went down in a flash of black cape, dingy petticoats, and scattered remedies and lurched off the rails on her knees.

Jack let go of the whistle chain and held his sides, laughing.

Chaldea bounded to her shoddy feet, gaped up at the engine and thrust a bony arm in the air. Two fingers arched out of a woolen mitten, wiggly as snakes poised to strike.

Daniel ducked to the floor.

Jack jerked him up again. "Crew's coming!"

To the west, men poured from the store. Daniel flung himself out after Jack. He missed a step on his way down. Jack broke his fall. They scrambled to their feet, grabbed their tree-tapping tools, and dashed into the timber just ahead of the train crew's garbled shouts.